NATIVE AMERICANS:

The New Indian Resistance

NATIVE AMERICANS:

The New Indian Resistance

by WILLIAM MEYER   *('yonv'ut'sisla)*

JAN 18 1973

INTERNATIONAL PUBLISHERS
New York

To D. Swift Bird

Library of Congress Catalog Card Number: 71-163221
ISBN 7178-0318-X
Printed in the United States of America

 X 565

CONTENTS

INTRODUCTION

SINCE THE alleged discovery of the Americas by Christopher Columbus in 1492, the native peoples of both North and South America have resisted the onslaught of colonialism. This colonialism has taken different forms depending on the nation perpetrating it, including the Spanish mission system, the French trade system, and the British settlement system. During the inter-colonialist wars in North America, the Indians fought on different sides because they were promised continued usage of their lands. Regardless of the agreements made with their white allies, they were never granted these rights very long. After the formation of the United States, the colonialism focused primarily on the land occupied by the numerous Indian nations, a continuation of the policy begun against them by the governments of the colonies. In order to halt this expansion, the Indians engaged in over 100 years of military resistance.

Another form of colonialism, certainly more insidious, has been the attempt by the Christian missionaries to take possession of the Indian soul. Catholics, Protestants, and Mormons have each sought to carve out their own little empires amongst the "fearsome heathens." This has been tried in most unappealing ways, not the least of which has been through legislation by the U.S. Congress.

The most recent form of colonialism has been the combined intrusion of federal agencies, missionaries, capitalists, industrialists, researchers, anthropologists, do-gooders, and tourists. The "Manifest Destiny" of the empire builders culminated in the invasion and subsequent defeat of the numerous tribes; reservations were established on the least useful land, opening a grim period for the Indians. Faced with the status of prisoners of war and overwhelmed by the regulations of the Bureau of Indian Affairs and the self-appointed agents of Euro-American civilization, the Indian resistance has taken on dynamic new forms of such subtlety that many people are not even aware that resistance is taking place.

The issues of current importance to the Indian movement are mostly old, unresolved, constitutional issues arising from treaties and rights guaranteed under treaties. Other issues center around the social consequences of the colonialist intrusions outlined above, particularly the irresponsible actions over the years by the Bureau of Indian Affairs.

However, there are underlying issues of even greater importance. These include the question of Indian national sovereignty, which is rooted in the earliest Indian-European treaties and the present, vital issue of Indian self-determination. Almost every local or tribal issue is related to these two goals. The increased propaganda by the government which tells us that all is well no longer rings true. The media have lied, as have the textbooks by which our children are educated.

The image of the Indians as presented to the American people is nothing short of slanderous. To so completely mislead the public about a segment of the people, and about the nation's history is exactly what America takes delight in accusing other nations of doing. No doubt it will surprise many people to know that there are over five million Americans of Indian descent and that the "Indian problem" was not "eliminated" a few years after the Battle of Little Big Horn. But, perhaps there is more to these distortions than slander. For a long time the conflicts and contradictions of the governmental spokesmen have been schizophrenic (defined as loss of contact with one's environment). One wonders whether contact was ever established with the American environment. The American Indian remains today as he has been in the past and is amazed at the willful destruction of the nation's resources.

This book does not presume to cover all the important issues nor to provide even a complete treatment of those included. The struggle of the Native American Church, for instance, has not been gone into, since it demands more thorough discussion than the space available allows. Nor have I spent as much time on the history of the early 20th century as I would have liked, presenting only a brief historical background. Immediate issues call for immediate presentation of the facts otherwise ignored in the news media. It is only fair that you hear the Indian side as you have already heard the government's, or perhaps have heard nothing. In the spirit of increased understanding, this indictment is submitted to you.

1

EUROPEAN COLONIAL PENETRATION

LET US begin with this fact: Columbus did *not* discover America. Can something be "discovered" which is already occupied by a considerable number of peoples with cultures attesting to no small degree of "civilization"? The narrow world view of the voyaging Europeans was arrogant, similar to the robust presumptions of Americans in the 20th century. The same blatant, overblown concept of self which was the heart and soul of the heroes of the "discovery" is also characteristic of those who today presume to police the entire world. Indeed, are they not descendants? Does exploitation justify the presumption of "discovery"? Hardly.

In 458 A.D. five Buddhist priests of Ki-piu (Afghanistan) are recorded in the Chinese Imperial Archives as having sailed from China to what was in all probability Alaska, California, and Mexico. After a lengthy visit seemingly verified by archeological discoveries of Oriental religious and artistic innovations among the Maya and Toltec Indians in Guatemala, they returned to China with a native shaman, who duly described the state of his coun-

try, and the advent of the Buddhist teachings among
his people. Elsewhere, Chinese artifacts used by
Indians have been discovered in British Columbia,
and Japanese-like pottery has been found in lo-
calities as far south as Ecuador. Records kept by
literate frontiersmen between 1779 and 1880 indicate that about 60 Japanese ships drifted onto the
West Coast of America, survivors coming ashore as
far afield as Sitka, Alaska and Santa Barbara on the
California coast. These shipwrecked seamen might
just as well have claimed the continent as anyone
else.

On the east coast of America the Norse seamen
made many attempts at settlement and trade over a
500 year period. During the 9th century Iceland was
used as a base for attacks upon Britain and Ireland.
Greenland was being colonized in the 11th century,
though with no apparent confrontation between the
Norse and the Eskimos, or "Skraelings," as Leif
Erickson's people named the North Americans
whom they encountered.

Norse expeditions reached Nova Scotia and Lab-
rador between 1007 and 1347 with considerable
warfare taking place between the Norse-Celtics and
the North American Indians. By the 14th century,
however, Greenland's Norse settlements were destroyed. In 1448, Pope Nicholas V wrote that sur-
prisingly the prisoners taken by the Indians were
freed after a time and returned to their homeland.
The implication is that he expected them to have
been forever enslaved. After all isn't slavery only
an institution practiced by pagans? In the 1490's
Pope Alexander VI commented that the former
Greenland Catholics, without a resident priest, must
surely have forgotten Christianity.

The presumptuous "discovery" of America by
Columbus can only be matched by the equally

unfounded theories on the origins of the Indians.*

Where did Indians come from? From Asia? Atlantis, maybe? Phoenicia perhaps? The Mormon religion claims we are one of the seven lost tribes of Israel, the Lamanites by name. Has anyone ever supposed that Indians might just possibly have their roots right in this hemisphere? It is likely that there were waves of immigration over the old Bering Strait during the Ice Ages, much like the Irish or Italian immigrations of more recent history. Boats may have drifted from the Pacific islands from time to time.

Why should it seem strange to most scholars that Indian nations have their own tales and histories of origins, migrations and the rise and fall of kingdoms (no less debatable than Biblical stories)? Among Indian people there are stories of continental origins, as well as stories about Oriental migrants who were assimilated into Indian society.

Let us examine the consequences of the "discovery." In the text books, much is made of Columbus' voyage to the Americas, and particularly the Island of San Salvador. Little is said of the genocide which he and future explorers practiced against the native populations of the Caribbean Islands. The facts are recorded elsewhere, however, far out of reach of the sensitive, undeveloped minds of our youth. I quote from the diary of Columbus, dated October 12, 1492: "It appears to me that the people are ingenious and would be good servants."

---

*At the time of writing, yet another group has claimed "discovery" rights to America. A spokesman for a Jewish scientific project suggests that as the Jews were escaping suppression in the Middle East, some of them arrived in what is now the Southeastern United States. Hebrew lettering, dating 1,000 years ago, on a stone in the Smithsonian is the evidence. It was found in Tennessee; more in Ohio.

And again, dated October 14: "These people are very unskilled in arms . . . with 50 men they could all be subjected and made to do all that one wishes." He also "ordered seven to be taken and carried to Spain in order to learn our language and return unless your Highnesses should choose to have them all transported to Castille or held captive in the Island." In a letter of the same date to Luis de Santangel, he wrote: " . . . to those (cotton, aloes, gold, spices, etc.) may be added slaves, as numerous as may be wished for."

Can one doubt the intentions thus expressed so few days after "discovering" the islands and the native people? There are many pages to Columbus' diary, and many books about those who administered the various islands over the next hundred or so years. They are all self-righteous chronicles of bloody, dishonorable events. Slave raids, rape, and murder led to uprisings, rebellion, and slaughter. Forced labor and starvation threatened the natural reproduction of the people. Suicides were frequent, as were self-induced abortions. There were mass executions by the Spaniards, as well as the individual tortures to while away the hours in the service of one's King. There were the epidemics to which the Indians had no natural immunity. Thus, from 1494 to 1496 the Indian population on the island of Hispanola (Dominican Republic and Haiti) diminished by a third from an estimated 500,000. By 1508, a census revealed that only 60,000 Indians remained. Four years later only 20,000 survived, and by 1548 Oviedo doubted whether 500 Indian people were alive.

Though different historians offer different figures for the genocide in the Caribbean, they do not question the fact of genocide. The islands now called Cuba, Puerto Rico, Jamaica, the Bahamas, and the Indies each suffered the same fate. So thorough was the genocide that soon Indians from the Mississippi valley and the Carolinas were being captured to fill the need for slave labor. When as a result of Indian resistance the supply of North American slaves was cut off, Africa began to be exploited to support the Spanish colonies.

It should not be thought that the native peoples did not resist the Spanish, for resist they did. The rebel leaders of the Caribbean fought a desperate battle for which they were not prepared. Records attest to the bravery of their struggle: Hathvey of Cuba, Caonaba of Hispanola, and others. The fight was at all times against weapons and a savage determination the Indians could not hope to equal, except by a great mass unification. In the Caribbean, as in South America, Mexico, and North America, this organization simply never came about. Thus, though he achieved momentary victories in battles, the Indian is always pictured losing the war.

The history of Peru as recorded by Prescott, and of Mexico under the Spanish and Catholic rulers is a repetition of much already mentioned. These advanced civilizations fell into disarray beneath the Spanish steel, horses, and smaller armies. The great Mexican forces had no chain of command, no supply lines, and only wooden weapons; thus an army of 200,000 men was subjugated by less than 600 Spaniards.

In Peru a colonial empire was ground out, though not without resistance. The long-armed Spanish rule was imposed no less viciously than the Inquisition itself. Wherever Catholic priests appeared, Indian religious worship was forbidden and religious leaders were tortured to death. This was more than mere religious persecution because political leaders were often also religious leaders. This fact was not known during the first conquests, but once realized it has been used again and again as a means of regulating Indian resistance. Indeed, to oppress our religion is to attack our entire community structure.

The Spanish sought to establish the mission system among the Pueblo Indians in the southwestern desert of North America. Communities were forced to settle around the mission in order to learn what the white "father" had to teach. He invariably taught forced labor, genocide, and great suffering. The pattern was the same from mission to mission.

Suppression, forced labor, religious persecution, starvation, rape—each led to rebellion. The Tarahumaras, Mayos, Yaquis, Zunis, Hopis, Rio Grande Pueblos, Apaches, Navahos, Yumans rebelled one by one. Each time they rebelled, the first thing they did was to kill the priest of the Catholic church, as just punishment for his Inquisitorial practices. Then the Indians would systematically kill all the overseers and colonialists in their region. Local governors would request the "law and order" forces, and the army would intervene, killing, slaughtering, and hanging all Indians in sight. Among the Tarahumaras, there were at least a dozen rebellions in which a total of over 10,000 Indians were killed in a period of perhaps 50 years. These do not include those killed as a result of disease, labor conditions, and the interruption of the normal birth cycles. The same pattern of resistance and oppression follows, for the Mayos and even more so for the Yaquis, whose resistance to foreign and colonial oppression is one of the most remarkable in the entire hemisphere. Next to the Yaquis, the Pueblos alone were reasonably successful in their resistance. In 1680 the Pueblos of the Rio Grande rebelled, successfully ridding themselves of Spanish rule for 18 years. No other single rebellion was as successful.

But Spain's day was running out. Unlike other colonial powers, Spain poorly spent the riches she extracted from the American colonies, squandering her wealth on courtly pleasures. She was soon a bankrupt power, unable to maintain herself in a rapidly commercializing world. Having drained and destroyed uncountable lives and resources, she was never able to reverse the tide. The whole history of Spain in the Americas is sadly like the parable of the goose and the golden egg. Nor were the other powers who soon sought to occupy America particularly generous. The Portuguese, more than any others, had the concept of slavery foremost in their minds. The Dutch, noted for their tulips and chocolate, were here noted for the introduction of scalping into the continent. No, scalping was not an Indian invention. It was introduced by the Governor of New Netherlands to facilitate collecting bounties on Indians. Once the Indians had assisted them in surviving the first few winters, the Dutch, hand in hand with the British, carried out a systematic program of genocide on all the eastern tribes.

Nor were the French different from their continental brothers. One of La Salle's first acts on his exploration was to make slaves of the Indians. The great heroes of the "discovery" and the "exploration" period of Euro-American history invariably showed neither respect nor civility toward those who welcomed them; almost to the man they were interested in the oppression and the exploitation of the Indians. The Russians were no different in their Alaskan explorations. Pushkarev's expedition, about 1760, established a pattern for the capture of slaves which remained unchanged for years.

It is not my intention to cover the entire pre-U.S. period. That has been done better elsewhere by other authors. It should be noted, however, that no complete history yet exists from the Indian viewpoint, which would be different, at least in terms of priorities, from those of other culture groups. Nor do I wish to dwell on the miscreant individuals who are everywhere praised for their conquest and genocide, for there is little to say concerning them that would be acceptable. May their souls rest.

Throughout the period of European colonialism the interests were mercantile-capitalist, and thus necessarily ruthless. The pity is that such base motivations ever should have been confused with those of religion, for no God ever justifies the ventures of exploiters. Nor is it likely that a God would sanction genocide, regardless of the presumed inferiority of the victim's soul. It is men who propose genocide, not Gods. Men contrive tyranny, and men oppose it. Greed passes from nation to nation, but is always in existence.

As the world revolves, boundaries of nations shift, monuments crumble and myths that we fabricate as objective history evoke in us emotions as far from reality as are our present national priorities. If you believe in the legends of Colonial Williamsburg (Virginia) or the Pilgrims of Boston or in the myth of the just and honest Quakers, or Father Washington, you may surely be surprised the day "they" come to take you away. Read for yourself the records of Cotton Mather, Grenville, Penn, and see if you can accept or justify their actions, particularly regarding Indians on whose land and resources they thrived. Finally, compare them with the world around you: the great democracy of America, built on obscenities, dishonor, racism, and hypocrisy. Must each reader continue to defend what is indefensible? Not for very much longer, brothers. Not for much longer.

Thus, America was "discovered," its inhabitants subjugated and the colonies settled, all in the name of progress which pollutes, of civilization which enslaves, and in the name of freedom to stomp on others as long as the law isn't around— and even if it is, if you are the right color and religion and can satisfy the judge.

2
EARLY EXPANSION OF
THE UNITED STATES

THE REVOLUTION by which the United States achieved independence was not a broad people's war. A relatively small number of immigrants actually took part in the fighting, and both sides used Indians to fight their battles for them. The majority of Indians, particularly among the Iroquois and Cherokee nations, sided with the English forces, primarily due to the dishonesty, brutality, and greed they had experienced at the hands of the American colonial insurgents.

The colonials were interested in land, regardless of whose it was or how long it had previously been occupied. On the other hand, the French had been more interested in the fur trade than in the acquisition of land. Since the success of fur trading depended on the Indian remaining an Indian, Indians were not converted to so-called "civilization," nor were they dispossessed from their lands. The Indians well understood the distinction between trade and settlement.

No matter which side the Indians supported, the new U.S. government presumed to rule over the Indian nations. The term, Indian "nation" should be understood in the same sense as a nation-state like France or the United States. It is a nation capable of self-government, law-making and enforcement and, most significantly, capable of entering into treaties with other nations. This view was early adopted by France, Spain, England and others in their relations with American Indians. The question of Indian national sovereignty persisted throughout the political dealings between the United States and the Indian people as the U.S. government constantly violated this sovereignty.

Our situation was analogous to that which would occur were Canada's parliament to pass a law to the effect that all U.S. citizens were subject to Canadian law. Whether or not it could enforce such a ruling, that ruling would be an unacceptable intrusion into the national sovereignty of U.S. citizens. So it was, and so it remains with American Indian nations. Each and every law passed by the United States to regulate the Indian nations has been just such an intrusion, each a presumption of the highest order, in which force has continually been needed to impose the illegal rulings. For centuries, before the "discovery" by the great European white fathers, we didn't need anyone to show us how to live on our land or govern ourselves.

In the Articles of Confederation, the United States presumed to "regulate the commerce between . . . the several . . . Indian tribes." During the drafting of the U.S. Constitution, this article was written into the section concerning Congressional powers. It was the sole provision on the new nation's relationship with the Indian nations. The Northwest Ordinance of 1787 extended governmental influence deeper into Indian affairs: "The utmost good faith shall always be observed towards the Indians, their lands and property shall never be taken from them without their consent; and in their property, rights, and liberty, they shall never be invaded or disturbed, unless in just and lawful wars authorized by Congress; that laws found in justice shall from time to time be made, for preventing wrongs done to them, and for preserving peace and friendship with them."

The Indian writer and member of the National

Indian Youth Council, Herb Blatchford, concludes an essay on this era of history with the Will Rogers quip, "When they pass a law it's a joke, and when they joke it's a law." But, Blatchford insists that the early laws of the struggling nation were sincere, and were intended to maintain peaceful relations with the still powerful Indian nations.

On this point I have deep doubts. I do not suppose that there was a conspiracy at the time aimed at extending the United States from coast to coast. But, everything points to the fact that the Republic intended to obtain as much land as quickly as possible from the Indians, honestly or otherwise. The stage had long been set for this expansion: the treaties for land cessions, such as the Penn "walking treaty" and a similar Long Island "walking treaty"; the practice of genocide whenever and wherever Indians were unwilling to part with their lands; the early establishment of Indian reservations by the Pilgrims following the King Phillip war.

The resistance by the Indians continued, not only to the new government, but to individual encroachments, and to the heavy-handed religious intrusions by the Christian missionaries. Sometimes the struggle assumed the proportions of a Holy War, which is exactly what it was. During the Pontiac rebellion just prior to the Revolutionary War, Lord Jeffrey Amherst, commander of the British forces, introduced germ warfare when he ordered the distribution of smallpox-infested blankets among the Indian camps. This rebellion, part of the French and Indian wars, ended with the death of Pontiac and another Indian defeat.

The United States began early to intimidate tribes into signing treaties which ceded vast areas of land. Where intimidation failed, there was always alcohol to demoralize and destroy the tribal power, and there were epidemics, which while not always deliberate were equally devastating, wiping out entire tribes. By the beginning of the 19th century American "Indian policy" was evolving as might be expected.

President Thomas Jefferson first proposed the removal of Indians from the eastern states to a region west of the Mississippi where they might continue to live, undisturbed by civilization. This program had a few drawbacks. First, the frontier was moving west faster than would prove safe for the removed Indians. Second, the Indians to be sent west would lose land, resources, and improvements which the government simply had no right to deprive them of by legislation. "Removal" began to be debated in 1802 and later became a popular policy.

In 1812 the Shawnees, like other tribes of the midwest, were continually harassed, threatened and conned into ceding their land. The government arbitrarily "appointed" several Indians as chiefs to represent their tribes in land cession treaties. In this manner the Sac and Fox tribes lost 50 million acres of land; the Delaware tribe lost three million acres, for which they were offered a mere $7,000. Many million acres were taken from dozens of other tribes. At times the government did not even wait for a treaty, but "extinguished" by legislation Indian title to occupied lands. The Shawnee tribe, under Tecumseh, rebelled against an illegal treaty, organized other Indians and urged the English to support them. Though the British captured the nation's capital, the Indian war was lost, and Tecumseh was killed. The Creek Indian wars followed a similar pattern. During this conflict Andrew Jackson introduced the "scorched earth" method of warfare. In the treaty of Fort Jackson at the war's end he stripped the Creek nation of all remaining eastern lands, thus preparing them for "removal."

When Jackson was elected President, the policy of Indian removal was on its way to becoming law. About this time the Department of Indian Affairs was established and was appropriately administered by the War Department, where it remained until 1849.

The policy of Indian removal was heatedly debated in the national press, as well as in state and federal legislative bodies. The debates sometimes threatened to tear apart the Union, as the issue of slavery did a few years later. The state of Georgia led the advocates for removal, and the Cherokee nation, so eager to progress in the white man's terms, was to be the first to suffer the consequences. When gold was discovered on Cherokee lands in northern Georgia, the greedy reprobates who had immigrated to Georgia from the European prisons would recognize no law greater than their own. The state of Georgia outlawed the Cherokee nation's right to self-government, and enforced their rulings by using vigilante groups. They killed and raped, and burned Indian farms and property, arresting and driving out sympathetic whites. When a case appeared before the Supreme Court in which Cherokee national sovereignty was reaffirmed, President Jackson was quoted as saying, "Now John Marshall has rendered his verdict, let him enforce it."

Indian removal became law in 1830. Cherokees, Creeks, Choctaws, Chickasaws and the handful of Seminoles who could be caught were rounded up and herded like animals over the "Trail of Tears" to Oklahoma. As many as 100 people a day died from exhaustion, starvation, and brutality at the hands of the U.S. Army. Indian property was auctioned to whites before the Indians were out of eyesight of their homes. Of the 50,000 Indians of the several tribes who made the forced march around one half perished. Yet in his report to Congress on the progress of Indian removal in December 1838, President Van Buren announced: "It affords me sincere pleasure to apprise the Congress of the entire removal of the Cherokee Nation of Indians to their new homes west of the Mississippi. The measures authorized by Congress at its last session have had the happiest effects. By an agreement concluded with them by the commanding general in that country, their removal has been principally under the conduct of their own chiefs, and they have immigrated without any apparent reluctance."

On their arrival in Oklahoma, those leaders of the Cherokee and Creek nations who signed the illegal treaties agreeing to removal were executed under the authority of the "Blood Laws" of the nations, which forbid any treaties selling or exchanging their lands. After years of intra-tribal strife over the illegal treaties, the U.S. government stepped in to mediate and at last to "reimburse" the tribes for the great sufferings imposed on them. But the tribes were forced to pay for their own removal out of the meager allowances held for them in the U.S. Treasury as payment for their stolen lands.

Only the resistance by the Seminole tribe to removal was relatively successful. The Seminole war waged by the U.S. Army cost the government $50 million with 1,500 men lost in the guerrilla fighting of the Everglades. Only a handful of Indians were taken, though every leader caught was murdered. Most leaders caught were captured while under a white flag of truce.

Eventually approximately 80 tribes were forced to resettle in Oklahoma territory. Boundaries established for one tribe were moved to squeeze in additional tribes. "Civilization" caught up to the removal lands almost before the tribes were resettled, but not before they had lost over 300 million acres of land to the speculators of the new "democracy." All the tribal governments were outlawed to prepare for Oklahoma statehood. Thus, the farce was completed.

3

WESTERN FRONTIER:
CIVIL WAR YEARS

AN ABRIDGED history may be as harmful as a distorted one, yet there are moments which epitomize the flux of nations. The resistance of the eastern Iroquois and the southern Cherokee held back the frontier for 150 years. Once they were muzzled, however, legislation and troops prodded the "frontier" westward at an alarming rate. In 1804, Lewis and Clark traversed the northern plains, setting foot in many areas as the first white men. The "frontier" at that time was considerably east of the Mississippi as far south as St. Louis. West of that was Indian land: first, the village tribes and on the plains, the plains tribes. All the territory from Canada into Mexico, 1200 miles deep from the Sierras east, was indisputable Indian country.

The tribes of the plains are not often portrayed as being friendly. Yet, they were not innately hostile to the foreigners, but merely cautious. After 300 years of hearing about the activities of white men among their compatriots, one wonders why they were even as open as they were. They had no idea that men would connive or conspire to obtain that which the Indians occupied, but themselves did not presume to own. Land ownership was as foreign to Indians as was genocide. Though the Indians are reputed to have waged centuries of inter-tribal war, and practiced torture and other "savage" acts, they never conceived nor practiced all-out, genocidal warfare. That fact has escaped most students of American and Indian history. Warfare between Indians was an acceptable, if dangerous pastime; it was a deadly game, played in earnest by one and all. The rules were strict, yet flexible—not so between white man and Indian. The rules were the white man's, as the Indians learned only after brutal losses, and then it was too late.

The history of the western frontier has an appeal to almost all people. The growing consciousness of the new country expanded onto the vast prairies, over the grand Rocky Mountains, and westward to the Pacific. The dash of the frontier, beyond the limitations of the "civilized" east, beyond law and order, still excites the American mind. Movies have consumed millions of feet of film recounting the adventures of one short century, of which only a fraction of the footage provides any theatrical action. The facts are distorted like those of the earlier "discovery" or are selected half-truths which are not substantially documented. The truth is less appealing than the fantasies by which Americans choose to live.

A young country must have heros and the west provided them. Names descend on us: George Armstrong Custer, Kit Carson, Buffalo Bill, and Generals Sheridan, Sherman and Crook. Other names are tucked away, such as Captain Fetterman and Colonel Chivington, whose honor have been sufficiently questioned to afford them relative anonymity. But, there were also Indian heroes, men whose statures loom tall against the colonial invasion: Sitting Bull, Crazy Horse, Gall, Red Cloud, Joseph, Two Moons, Dull Knife, Satanta, Scarface Charlie, Captain Jack, Cochise, Geronimo, Mangas Colorado, Victorio, Nachez, and innumerable others. This is the stuff of epics and of dreams turned off like a light.

The uprisings near the Mississippi, the Pontiac

and Tecumseh wars, the Black Hawk war (in which Honest Abe Lincoln fought), the general struggle against land theft and encroachments—all revealed to the Indians that resistance was nearly futile. The settlers kept pressing, the missionaries kept Christianizing and the government, having created "wards of his Indian children," continued to come late with the annuities on which his new wards survived. A promise made was a promise soon broken. The records of every Congressional investigation held on the Indian question make amusing reading.

The Minnesota uprising of 1862 by the Sioux Indians was a just retaliation for such interference. After 50 years of making treaties with the United States, these Sioux had a reservation ten miles by 50 miles from an original 30 million acres. Most of the land had been acquired at a nickel an acre by sharp government agents. For this land they received money, goods and food. The money went to the quick-witted traders with their "double-entry" ledgers, and the goods were rarely what the treaty specified. The food was unbearable, but the Indians were "allowed" to go on an annual buffalo hunt after their annuities were paid. White settlers had even begun to encroach on their greatly reduced reservation, even though there was a federal law against squatting.

In 1862 the annuities were late. Without the food gained from hunting, the Sioux were sure to starve. An incident with a squatter over one chicken resulted in a shoot-out in which five settlers were killed. The Sioux were certain, however, that the entire tribe would be held responsible for the deaths. They decided upon an attack on the Agency office and the white community before the army could be mobilized. Led by Chief Little Crow, the attack was successful, and other raids followed.

Yet, the Sioux were certain that success would only be temporary, and that in the end the survivors would be subjected to severe punishment. Indeed, once the Minnesota Regulars led by Colonel Sibley entered into action, the Sioux offensive was halted and their forces defeated.

Most of the Indians who had taken part in the uprising, particularly in the early stages of the actual massacre, retreated into the Dakotas. Those remaining, who had very little reason to run, were rounded up to be tried in Sibley's court. The death penalty was ruled valid if a man could be proven present during a battle. Killing or other crimes were not necessary to achieve the death penalty. The court would convict a man to the gallows in as brief a time as five minutes. Within one month 306 Indians out of 400 were condemned to death. Another 16 were given prison sentences. Seventeen hundred Indians, mostly women and children, were taken and held at Fort Snelling, subjected to abuse from whites during their march as though they had been the warriors. The condemned men were taken in chains to Mankato prison and were set upon by wild mobs as they passed through angry settlements.

Only direct intervention by President Lincoln at the request of Episcopalian Bishop Whipple reduced the number of condemned to 38. These men were swiftly hung and then buried in a mass grave, their bodies "borrowed" by local doctors for their medical investigations. Indian graves, new and old, are always open to speculation. The remaining prisoners were set on by zealous Christian missionaries, "successfully" converted, and removed to a yet smaller reservation.

The Minnesota uprising was the beginning of the period of the Plains Indian Wars from 1862–1891, which eventually involved most of the tribes west of the Mississippi. In the early 1860's, the west was divided into numerous tribal territories. On the northern plains were the Sioux, Mandans, Hidatsas, Crows, Cheyennes, and Arapahos. Throughout the northern Rockies and to the west were the Flatheads, the Nez Percé, Coeur d'Alenes, and Shoshones. On the northwest coast were the Columbia river tribes, too numerous to list. South of these were the numerous California tribes and Indian communities who had suffered under Spanish and Mexican rule. To the east and into the great Basin of Nevada and Utah were the Paiutes. In what is now Arizona and New Mexico were the Pueblos, Navahos, Apaches, Mohaves, Pimas, Papagos and many smaller tribes of desert Indians. On the southern plains were the Comanches, Kiowas and Kiowa Apaches, as well as the Cheyennes, Arapahos, and Sioux. In the southern Rockies were the Utes.

For the most part the Plains had not been the scene of persistent Indian resistance, for the United States had bypassed the Plains in its haste to expand onto the west coast. The one major exception were the Apache wars with the Spanish during their period of occupation of the southwest. The Mormons had actually attempted to ally with the Plains tribes in a far-fetched military scheme to gain control of the Pacific northwest from the whites who had settled there. The powerful Nez Percé held back on the alliance, thus sabotaging the Mormon dream.

Certainly, the white westward migration would hardly be halted by means of alliances with white groups. Trails to the west cut across buffalo hunting grounds; railroad companies needed land on which to lay their tracks. It is true that federal laws existed to protect Indian rights, but the U.S. army never enforced them. When the Indians took up arms to defend their lands, hunting rights and families, the army defended the white settlers from these "savages." The constant changeover of U.S. administrations, brought with it evershifting policies and programs for "civilizing" the Indians, which simply meant to settle them on smaller areas of land, so that the white man could have the rest. Often, it was this continual shifting of programs which alone was responsible for precipitating wars. The army suppliers and teamsters, the military-industrial complex of the 19th century, were known to have incited both Indians and whites to wars for their own short-sighted benefits.

Propaganda depicting Indians as symbols of ignorance as against the great, white progress of immigrant Americans is racist, as is the portrayal of Indians as undirected or misdirected savages causing suffering merely for the hell of it. They were fighting to protect their lives, lands, and food supplies (buffalo) from willful destruction by the mindless white man. I say "willful" because of the slick public relations job done to urge homeless immigrants into areas yet unsettled. And I say "mindless" because, as with the present U.S. foreign policy and space program, there was relatively little foresight regarding the "progress" so long flaunted as a positive product of America's growth.

The first great acts of occupation of the Plains territory occurred in the early 1860's. The U.S. government seized several million acres in the Oklahoma Territory, mostly from the several tribes "removed" there. Funds for the land were held in the U.S. treasury, but were reduced by fines against the Indians. Personal property, such as horses and cattle, was taken from the Indians "to teach them a lesson," one which they already knew well.

At the same time, the Southern Plains Indians were pressured by homesteaders and prospectors. As a result, these Indians were dispossessed onto a small reservation in southeastern Colorado. Unable to sustain their livelihood on the reservation, the Indians raided outlying areas in search of food. The U.S. army, in turn, encouraged raids on "peaceful" Indian camps by offering the captured stock as a reward to the soldiers. The more frequent occurence of raids threatened to break out into full scale war. The Governor of Colorado, John Evans, ordered all Indians to set up camp at the nearest fort as a sign of their "peaceful intentions." He declared that any tribe refusing to do so would be considered hostile. Obviously, this tactic could justify any future military actions against the "hostile" Indians. In truth, Evans had long been of the opinion that only an Indian war would solve the Indian question.

The army proceeded to harass those Indians who had camped near the forts in the hope of avoiding conflict. As the only alternative, a general council of Southern Plains Indians opted for all-out war. They designed a coordinated military strategy, which in many respects resembled the strategy of guerrilla warfare. The war spread north to the Sioux and south to the Comanches and the Kiowas. The Comanches, taking advantage of the Texan involvement in the Civil War, carried the conflict into that state. Governor Evans sent messages to Washington accusing the Indians from Canada to Texas of a conspiratorial alliance. He issued orders for citizens "to go in pursuit . . . also to kill and destroy as enemies . . . wherever they might be found, all hostile Indians."

A section of Cheyennes under Black Kettle still sought peace, even going to Denver to confer with Governor Evans. However, the Governor and the military commander, General Curtis, remained uninterested in overtures of peace. The Cheyennes withdrew to Fort Lyons, but were refused camping permission. They finally set up camp at Sand Creek.

One day later, on November 28, 1864, Sand Creek was the scene of a massacre of the Cheyennes by the Third Regiment of the Colorado Volunteers under Colonel Chivington. Chivington instructed his men: "Kill and scalp all, big and little; nits make lice." The butchery of the Chivington massacre at Sand Creek, though only one of many, many similar actions rarely recorded in genteel textbooks, was unequaled by Indian "savages" anywhere or any time during their resistance to the advance of white "civilization." Women were shot down while pleading for mercy. Other women were cut down with sabers and otherwise mutilated, to be left alive in lieu of more lively quarry. Children carrying white flags were slaughtered and pregnant women were cut open. The slaughter and mutilation continued into the late afternoon over many miles of the bleak prairie. Genitals were later exhibited by the victors as they marched into Denver, and some were made into tobacco pouches.

The camp had contained nearly 1,000 Indians. Though reports vary as to the number killed, the generally accepted figure of nearly 200 still stands, of whom about 150 were women and children. The Denver *News* reported that "All (soldiers) acquitted themselves well." Only three women and four children were taken prisoner and exhibited like caged animals in Denver. Great applause was given the men displaying their Indian scalps between acts in the Denver theatres.

The massacre did not pass without its political repercussions. A military investigation uncovered much evidence against Chivington. As a result Congress voted to grant reparations to the widows and orphans of the massacre, a "generous" gesture considering that most of the dead were women and children.

For the Southern Plains Indians, the Sand Creek massacre only served further to unify their ranks and to dismiss any notion of a peaceful settlement. Their fighting organization was able to resist a force of 8,000 U.S. troops, supplied at a cost of $30 million. During all of 1865 the Indians lost a total of only 20 fighters. In spite of the tenacity of the resistance, various government commissions unilaterally decided that the Cheyennes, and their allies as well, must give up the remaining lands of their traditional domains, and accept a reservation. But Congress refused to ratify the new agreements, forcing these tribes to roam for several years with no land to call their own.

4

WESTERN FRONTIER:
POST-CIVIL WAR YEARS

FOLLOWING THE Civil War, westward expansion took an even more aggressive turn. The era of transcontinental railroads was beginning, in which 175 million acres of land were to be given to companies as rights of way, and later would be sold by these companies for a tidy profit. Much of the land throughout the west was Indian land, unpurchased and unceded. Also during this period, a method of commercially tanning the buffalo hide was invented, and what had previously been merely a sport to shoot the shaggy beasts from train and carriage windows, albeit with the company's approval and the urging of army commanders, now became justified slaughter in the name of free enterprise. As the railroads were pushed through Indian country, they divided the herds of buffalo, allowing for easier elimination. The herds were reduced by 50 million by about 1885. An Indian in Wyoming, having obtained and raised several buffalo calves, in later years sold them to the government in order to prevent their total extinction.

Government policy was to reduce the land holdings of the tribes through treaties. While the soldiers of the Confederacy were given mules and land with which to become farmers, the Indians were pushed further into the western "frontier." The resistance of the Southern Plains Indians had been undercut by enormous plagues of smallpox and cholera, and by the increased use of alcohol at the treaty councils. At Medicine Lodge Creek in Kansas the Comanches, Kiowas, and Southern Cheyennes and Arapahos signed treaties in which they accepted reservations in Indian Territory, as Oklahoma had been briefly named before its statehood. Thus, the remaining tribes along the Mississippi were being neatly shipped off to Indian territory. In addition, the Colorado Utes agreed to a reservation in the Colorado Rocky Mountains.

Everywhere the government was pressing the Indians to give up their centuries-old life-styles and to adopt white ways on the barren reservations. As an "anecdote" in the perennial corruption in the Indian Bureau, President Grant initiated the Quaker or Peace Plan. Various denominations were given the right to run the reservations in a Christian manner. Thus, there began a new inquisition of Indian religious practices, by which medicine men could be convicted of "religious crimes" and imprisoned.

Although the Southern Plains Indians had submitted to the treaties, the Northern Plains Indians further resisted the occupation of their territories by the U.S. Army and the transformation of their lands into a right of passage for the railroads. As early as 1866, the U.S. Army began to construct a line of forts along the Boseman Trail in Montana. Railway roadbeds were to be built alongside the trail earlier beaten by wagons. The trail penetrated through the hunting territory of the powerful Teton Sioux. During the summer of 1866, the Sioux mounted an offensive against the troops that were building the forts. By the spring of 1867, Forts Reno, Kearney, and Smith were under permanent seige.

In April 1868, the Peace Commission signed a treaty with the Oglala, Brule, Hunkpapa, Miniconjou, and Yanktonais Sioux and the Arapaho in which the Indians agreed to accept reservations, but retained the right of the hunt "so long as the buffalo may range in numbers sufficient to justify the chase." Yet most of the Sioux did not accept this treaty, holding out until the Bozeman Trail was closed. In May of that year the trail was ordered closed, and in August the forts were abandoned. Each fort was burned by the Indians as the troops marched away, leaving only the cemeteries behind.

In the treaty Red Cloud finally signed that November, the Bighorn country was given the status of unceded Indian land, forbidden to whites, and to be forever available to the several tribes who defended it.

This clear-cut military victory only served as a temporary setback to U.S. expansion into the territory of the Northern Plains Indians. The next ten years brought with them continual conflicts, each battle further weakening the Indian resistance. These battles stand out in even the most "genteel" textbooks: the Battle of Beecher Island; the Battle of the Washita, or "Custer's First Stand" (where he made errors repeated in his "Last Stand"); the Battle of Adobe Walls during the Red River war; the Battle of Palo Duro Canyon; the Sappa River Massacre; the Modoc War in Oregon; the Bighorn Campaign of 1876; Chief Joseph's battles; the Cheyenne's attempt to return North.

With the end of the Northern Plains wars, it was decreed that any Indians remaining off reservations would be considered hostile to the U.S. government. Eventually the last groups, led by Sitting Bull and Crazy Horse, came in, and were duly assigned to reservations. Yet intrigues continued, leading to the assassination of Crazy Horse in 1877. Sitting Bull was killed during a ridiculous attempt to arrest him during the suppression of the Ghost Dance religion in 1890.

In the southwest, the Navaho and the Apache

stood in the way of the search for gold and other minerals by U.S. prospectors. After the Spanish mission system was discontinued, a system which destroyed most Indian cultures, the Southwest Indians were thrown upon the mercy of the greediest, least humane element of American citizenry. It was said that throughout the southwest, including California, no white man ever did any work for himself if there were Indians around. Indian slaves were used by government officials, priests, and others, to be discarded when they could work no more. Numerous plans were proposed to "resettle" the Navaho and Apache, turn them into good farmers and Christians and steal their excess land. Just as the Indians began to adjust to one program, it was discontinued, and a new one, often exactly the opposite, was substituted. This administrative indifference to the conditions of the Indians still infests the management, if one could call it that, of the Indian Bureau.

The U.S. government began its colonial assault against the Southwest Indians in 1863 when Kit Carson was assigned the task of subduing the Navaho. He did so by means of "scorched earth" warfare, employing perhaps even more gruesome tactics against women and children than used at Ash Hollow, Blue Water Creek, Sank Creek, and other notable U.S. army battles waged against women.

The Apaches, however, displayed a fiercer resistance. In 1863 Cochise and Mangas Colorado initiated a war against both the United States and Mexico. Both country's armies were hard-pressed to control their activities. The Mexicans were offering $100 for an Apache scalp in 1863. But, Apaches did not always give up their own hair so willingly, and many less fierce Indians were not given a choice. An Apache leader caught was as sure as dead. Mexican soldiers captured Mangas Colorado under a flag of truce, tortured him with a heated bayonet, and shot him down when he tried to escape. The U.S. authorities pursued a policy of constant relocation of the Apaches from one reservation to another. This policy further disturbed those Indians who had been willing to settle on reservations. Whole tribes would rejoin the war after several shifts in their "permanent" homes. Apache leaders like Victorio, Geronimo and Nachez repeatedly succeeded in maneuvering their tribes off the reservations in order to continue the resistance.

Finally by 1885, the active Apache forces had been reduced to 100 warriors. An elite desert corps was dispatched to eliminate them. In one surrender of 77 Apaches to General Crook, only 15 were men. They were all sent into exile to Florida prisons. Geronimo and Nachez surrendered, with conditions, and were sent directly to Florida. President Cleveland, uninformed of the conditional nature of their surrender, spoke of the coming war crimes trials he intended to hold, presuming the right before trial to hang Geronimo and Nachez. There was a general roundup of Apaches in Arizona. Forced exile in Florida under extreme conditions insured the death of most of the 600 Apaches there.

By 1886, with all the reservations established and with the fighting more or less concluded, there began the final phase of Indian injustices. In a way, this phase is the more important one in the relationship of Indians to the United States. In the actions of the years following the wars, the Americans revealed themselves to be as repressive, destructive and narrow as their war tactics had demonstrated they were.

Once imprisoned on the reservations, the Indians were at the mercy of every politician, trader, missionary, and foolish do-gooder that the imagination can conceive. It was government policy to keep Indians undernourished. It was government policy to take six-year-old children from their parents, cut their hair nice and short, and send them away to so-called boarding schools in which they were taught meaningless foreign subjects and were brutally punished for minor infringements of rules or for speaking their own languages. The overcrowded conditions and the poor food at the schools led to epidemics and early deaths. The schools became breeding grounds for diseases that were later carried home and spread on the reservations. All this was well known to the administrators of the Indian programs. Children were expected to die, and those who survived were expected to no longer be "blanket" Indians. Indian religions were outlawed, to be crushed and stamped out at the missionaries' request. As recently as the 1930's, religious suppression was encouraged; "Give Christianity a chance," demanded fascist missionary George W. Hinman. These practices were a mere portion of the American rehabilitation programs.

In 1887 the Dawes Act was enacted, known to us as the Land Allotment Act. At this time Indians still nominally owned in the neighborhood of 150 million acres of land. It was decided that they couldn't possibly become farmers unless each Indian had his own little plot of that land. The real intention behind the Act, however, was more to the point. The land was still owned by tribes, rather than the good-old-American-individual-ownership way. Tribal land was the base for tribal power. It was decided to further destroy the tribal structure by individualizing land holdings; each Indian head of family received a plot. After allotment, whatever land remained reverted back to the United States. Out of the 150 million acres before allotment, 90 million acres went unallotted. Through a simple legislative theft, these lands were forever lost to the Indians. What remained was essentially 60,000,000 acres of eroded acreage, and a severely weakened tribal structure.

Then began a wonderful series of programs, each evoking laughter from the saddened Indians. These programs were designed to fail economically, but tribes were occasionally able to make them work. Some cattle raising ventures were successful, but when they did work, they were considered competitive threats to the white cattlemen, and forcibly discontinued. Forestry ventures were ruined, or turned over to white lumbering concerns. Irrigation projects paid for by Indians only benefited the whites who leased Indian land. Oil was discovered on certain Indian reservations, but the padded bills and raised prices on Indian-purchased items devoured entire fortunes. The Indian agent was always ready, able and corrupt. The missionary was always urging his parishioners to save themselves from the hell of heathenism. The churches received millions of dollars from the trust funds of illiterate Indians.

Thus, the cessation of military genocide in the last decade of the 19th century led to the application of more subtle genocidal techniques—techniques which have been used continuously to this present day. Yet, only by understanding the historical resistance of the Indian, can one come to grips with the demands of the Indian rights movement, for it is on the basis of rights that were guaranteed by the U.S. government before the 20th century that these demands are formulated. Only then will the continuity of Indian resistance be made clear.

5

BUREAU OF INDIAN AFFAIRS: SOCIAL GENOCIDE

DURING THE 20th century, the exploitation of the Indians has become more extensive. Every aspect of Indian affairs has become fair game for the colonialist forces. These forces represent a cross-section of U.S. society: the federal government; the agencies of the federal, state, and local governments; academic and Christian institutions; financial foundations; industries, including oil, lumber and paper, mineral (coal, uranium, etc.), and elements of the military-industrial complex; arts and crafts exploitation; "traders," tourists and the recreation industry; unions which refuse to allow certain Indian industries; the judicial and law enforcement agencies; the film and television industries; and just about every non-Indian group which comes into contact with Indians and continues to exploit Indians for everything it can extract. Far from protecting the Indians, a role assumed at the outset by the U.S. government, it is the source of the greatest exploitation. Furthermore, governmental efforts are diluted and confused by the continuing involvement of all the other groups.

41

The Bureau of Indian Affairs (BIA) coordinates and administers the federal programs for the reservations. Moved from the Department of War to the Department of Interior in 1849, it is the least profitable of Interior's bureaus, and conflicts with many other priorities. The Department of Interior has been traditionally riddled with graft and corruption, and the Bureau of Indian Affairs has long institutionalized these virtues. All transactions between Indian wards and non-Indians are regulated at the whim of the Interior Department and the BIA. All land leases and sales are with the strict guidance of these agencies, as are the settlement of wills and estates. Thus the vested interests of forestry, mining, and non-Indian farmers and ranchers are in the best position to negotiate through the Indian Bureau.

Needless to say, other governmental departments have even higher priority. Since the U.S. Army and the Army Corps of Engineers can wield the legal power to condemn property, they have easy and frequent access to Indian lands, for practice-firing and bombing ranges and for the atrociously short-sighted projects for the construction of dams.

Indians have little to say regarding their own property or services. The BIA runs their schools, and the Public Health Service operates a few clinics and hospitals. Therefore, Indians have no voice in their own education and health facilities. Whenever they openly attempt to oppose government programs and actions, pressures are brought down on them which cause the loss of the few jobs available. Often, violence is used to quiet the "troublemaker." The Indians, due to their special status, have no recourse to the American judicial system, unless the Interior Department approves, which it rarely does. The government uses other means of keeping the Indians quiet as well. Indian funds for lands and claims settlements are kept on deposit with the U.S. Treasury in what are cynically called "trust" funds. The government can freeze funds at any time it desires. Also, the government may legislate to "terminate" its relationship with a tribe, thereby cancelling further assistance, and removing the status of Indian lands from the tax-free category. The cases in which this has occurred invariably have proved to be economic disasters for the tribes. Thus, Indians placed at the mercy of the conquerers still remain in that position today.

The American Indians, defeated and then utterly oppressed, decreased in population until, in the first years of the 20th century, there were only 250,000 Indians remaining in the United States out of an original population estimated at 12 million. Since the first decade, however, the population has stabilized and then increased. Yet, nowhere in the many investigations and hearings do we hear mentioned the decimation of the Indian population. Apparently this slaughter was a policy of war, and war is not really violence, or rather it is justifiable violence.

Again and again must be repeated the statistics of Indian poverty and Indian genocide in America today. Life expectancy of a reservation Indian is 43 years; only 33 in Alaska and Arizona. Infant mortality is twice that of the rest of America. We have a 50 per cent high school dropout rate. A student finishing a BIA school has the education equal to that of the eighth grade elsewhere in America. Jobs simply do not exist on the reservations. Unemployment may be normally as high as 75 per cent. Where industries have been established their aim is to employ women rather than men, except lumbering, mining and the like. A large number of missile and rifle manufacturing plants have found their way onto reservations, in support of America's war efforts. The yearly earnings of most reservation families fall far below the national level of poverty, which is $1500. Few families actually earn that much. Only government-employed Indians do, as do the few who have progressed in the white man's terms. The remainder earn as little as $l50 a year. Thus many are forced to fall back on the traditional methods of living off the land: gathering vegetables and fruits, fishing, and hunting. One of the major issues of recent struggles revolves around the right to hunt, to fish, and to gather food, as provided, or not implicitly signed away, in the treaties.

Most reservations are still shrinking in size as non-Indians buy up heirship lands. The heirs to anyone's land are sent a form from the BIA, asking them to sign it if they want to sell. The poor administration of Indian heirship lands has produced an unimaginable monster in which one acre of land may be owned by as many as 200 individuals, none of them retaining the right to use the land, but granting the BIA and Department of Interior rights to lease the land as they see fit. This means in practically all cases that it will be leased to a non-Indian for five, 25, or perhaps even for 99 years. Thus an Indian, rather than receiving the absurd lease checks for $1.80 a year or a similar amount, may well sign away his land. It doesn't really seem to be his anyway. The government slowly obtains the signatures of all the owners, and the land may be sold. It is almost never purchased by Indians. Thus only seven reservations, to my knowledge, are expanding in size, while all the rest are diminishing. The land base continues to be stolen, though presumably all is now legal.

Pine Ridge reservation in South Dakota, the second largest Indian reservation in the United States, is one of those that is shrinking. The U.S. Army has aided this process immensely. In the early years of World War II, one-quarter of it was condemned for use as an aerial-gunnery range, with the understanding that the land would revert to the tribe after the war. It did not, and was not classified as "surplus" land until the late 1960's. A bill finally passed Congress in favor of the Pine Ridge Sioux, but only after the Department of Interior had classified the "surplus land" as part of the National Park domain, so it then could be leased to white cattlemen should the Sioux be unable to re-purchase it. Thus the Pine Ridge reservation is divided due to land sales which were forced on the Indians by a BIA anxious to maintain the Sioux as a nation in poverty, and assisted by the U.S. Army and the Department of Interior. Pine Ridge today is barely half Indian owned.

The positive efforts of some tribes, notably the Cheyenne River tribe of Sioux, have solved the problems of poor land administration by a program of consolidation of heirship lands, thereby reducing the number of individuals owning a single plot of land, and bringing together several pieces of property owned by an individual as a result of heirship regulations. They have thus made their lands more usable to members of the tribe, and have begun to purchase unused lands in the name of the tribe itself. The program has proved successful; the landbase of this tribe is continually expanding, and is becoming a model for other tribes throughout the country.

More recent administrative fiats of the BIA have further reduced the Indian land base. Termination is the policy of granting the Indians the promise of independence, while removing Indian lands from the non-tax status, thereby putting new pressures on the tribes. This policy was developed under the Eisenhower Administration, with the plan itself originating from Secretary of Interior Dillon S. Myer. Mr. Myer came well equipped to the Bureau of Indian Affairs. During World War II, he had served as head of the Oriental Relocation Authority under which 100,000 Japanese-Americans were herded into concentration camps on the west coast, several camps on Indian reservations! In a series of unprecedented bills presented to Congress, he almost succeeded in eradicating the more positive actions of the previous 20 years. His bills included plans to remove all Indian land from the trust (non-tax) status, to repeal the Indian Reorganization Act, to outlaw 100 tribal constitutions, to outlaw 200 tribal corporations, and to introduce "termination." He was removed from office, but not before seven tribes were terminated.

The Menominee tribe in Wisconsin was the most harmed by these new laws. The self-sufficient Menominee tribe owned a sustained-yield lumber operation, which employed most of the men, provided health and education for all and covered all welfare costs. When termination was imposed, the lumber mill, unable to provide for the increased tax load, was automated, and serious unemployment ensued. Land had to be sold for tax purposes. Ten years later, Menominee County was one of the 10 most depressed in the United States.

The Army Corps of Engineers, with the full cooperation of the BIA, has repeatedly built dams in the name of reclamation which have flooded valuable reservation lands. Perhaps few people are aware that a dam, though the actual structure is built to last for centuries, only functions to its full capacity for 50 years. Expensive and often impossible dredging operations extend their life only another 10 years. This is due to the tons of siltage and wastes which accumulate in the reservoir at a rate of one to six per cent every year. With huge quantities of water gathered behind certain dams, there is the problem of evaporation. Lake Mead, to name only one, loses more water to evaporation every day than now flows into it, thus cancelling out one of its main purposes.

Flood control is not a valid reason to destroy the ecology of a river with a dam. The North Dakota floods of 1969 occurred in spite of the Garrison Dam, a dam which had previously destroyed the landbase and economy of the Fort Berthold Indian reservation by flooding one-quarter (154,000 acres) of its rich bottom lands. Into the bargain, it had caused them the loss of substantial oil revenues. Due to the Garrison Dam, the Department of Interior and the Army Corps, the Fort Berthold people, once completely self-sufficient (they required only $5,000 a year for welfare prior to the dam), now are 60 per cent unemployed and demoralized, and require $573,000 in welfare payments to barely survive.

The Lake of Perfidy, behind the Kinzua dam, floods 10,000 acres of land which the Seneca Nation of New York State was ensured of never losing in a treaty with George Washington. During the hearings on this dam, the Senecas hired their own engineers who proved that the dam could be built more cheaply and serve the same purpose if placed about 30 miles downstream. The Army Corps, which receives open-ended funding from the Congress, doesn't care about saving money. The dam was built, forcing the Senecas to relocate an entire town. The relocation paid for by the United States, was determined along religious lines, with the Christianized Indians receiving first choice in new lots and housing. The traditional Handsome Lake followers of the Longhouse were forced to accept isolated lots and in most cases have had to build their own houses. Officials have now deemed the dam inadequate and have proposed plans to build another in the near future.

When the Yellowtail dam in Montana was built, the Crow Indian reservation received no compensation for their rights, either to land or water. There are 40 more cases just like this one.

The Navaho tribe was drawn into an irrigation project in 1963, that was to be partly beneficial to themselves, and partly to non-Indian farmers just off the reservation. Although their money was put into the project, by 1965 only the non-Indian part was completed, while today the Navaho have no water for their fields. The same has been reported at Zuni, Yuma, Paiute, and Papago reservations of the southwest, as well as among several northern reserves already mentioned in relation to other governmental thefts.

These numerous transactions, along with the policy of termination, are the product of public servants who work for private interests. They use terms such as "for the good of the nation," and "in the best interest of the Indians," and they have usurped the power to regulate Indian land and rights, which supposedly can be done only with the Indian's consent. Well-documented sources show that Indians are not consulted and not even informed of thefts after they occur. Nor is the Bureau of Indian Affairs the so-called guardians of Indian estates, exactly honest. On one trip to a South Dakota reservation the Bureau's industrial development officer admitted to thefts from the previous reservation he had represented (Qualla, North Carolina Cherokee) and went on to brag of his thefts of $18,000 from the Pine Ridge funds. "I have five children to put through college," he said. He was later transferred away from Pine Ridge—civil servants are rarely fired.

The documentation of social genocide does not begin to tell the story of the life and death of today's

Indian people. It does not reveal the racism surrounding Indian reservations and communities, nor the racism built into the BIA, nor the racist policemen just waiting to catch an Indian drunk, particularly a young Indian girl. You may think that this doesn't happen in present-day America. I suggest that this does happen, that few white men who today murder an Indian will stand trial for it, and that it is all but certain no jury will convict them should a trial occur. Yet Indians populate the jails in western states. In Idaho, where the Indian population is perhaps 10,000, 68 per cent of all prisoners are Indians. In other states, such as South and North Dakota, Colorado, New Mexico, and Arizona it is between 35 and 50 per cent. Their crimes are drunkenness, loitering, minor thefts, but rarely felonies; certainly their crimes are not land theft, genocide, or assassination of government leaders. Sometimes it is hard to believe that they are not. They serve sentences just as long.

6

LAND AND WATER RIGHTS

IN THE original treaties with the various Indian nations, the U.S. government guaranteed these nations the possession and utilization of both land and water. Under the terms of the treaties the federal government was legally obligated to protect Indian possessions from violations by private citizens and state and local authorities. Needless to say, the government has failed to provide this protection. Many times the federal government has itself violated the treaty rights. Currently, numerous tribes are waging legal battles for control over their rightful lands and waters. The following cases are only a sampling of many legal struggles.

The Paiutes

In the Nevada desert, water is more valuable than even gold. In a nation of rapidly diminishing supplies of fresh water for industry and individual consumption, "old" treaties (as treaties are called when they stand in the way of non-Indians) which guarantee rights to specific rivers and lakes become political issues overnight. Justice may turn on the tides like a piece of driftwood.

Pyramid Lake is cupped amid rolling hills and the sprawling desert of western Nevada. When it was "discovered" by Captain John Fremont in 1844, he considered it to be more beautiful than nearby Lake Tahoe. The lake was filled with fish, including the now extinct prehistoric fish, Cui-ui. The lake was not wanted by the white men, nor were the surrounding lands; thus, by a treaty in 1859, both lake and lands were deeded to the Paiute tribe living there. However, under the presidency of Theodore Roosevelt, the Interior Department began to exercise their prerogatives in the name of conservation. A dam was built on the Truckee River to divert water to the Interior Department's own Newlands Irrigation Project, thereby taking huge quantities of water away from Pyramid Lake. The project was designed to make 287,000 acres of land irrigatable, though to date only a quarter of this goal has been accomplished due to the loss of 65 per cent of the water to evaporation and seepage in the unlined ditch-system.

In 1930 the Paiutes discovered that the number of trout and other fish had decreased almost to extinction. The Derby Dam had cut off the fish from their accustomed spawning grounds, and the lake itself was drying up, one to two feet a year, due to the decreased flow of water. BIA employees who sympathized with the tribe and attempted to assist it in the legal battles to regain the water were fired or given assignments far away from the Paiute reservation. Nevertheless, the tribe won several court cases concerning their rights to the water being diverted.

Today, it has been acknowledged that the Derby Dam diversion removes far more water than it needs, water that is used elsewhere for a sportsmen's preserve, or merely run off into the desert to evaporate. The Interior Department's answer has been to propose the building of new dams, which the Indians have successfully opposed. The Department has promised many things while secretly revising the rules and regulations of the Newlands Project so that the lake will receive none of the excess water.

In 1969 came the newest threat: the California-

Nevada Compact, which would effectively subordi-
nate Indian water rights to those of the states. The
Compact's effect on Pyramid Lake would be even
more immediate. California would benefit from the
Compact by receiving water from the Truckee
River diversion, thus cutting down the flow into
Pyramid from an already inadequate 275,000 acrefeet* to a mere 30,000 acrefeet a year. It is known
that in order to stabilize the sinking lake at its
present size (107,000 acres) it would require an
increase to 363,000 acrefeet of water a year. Not
only are the remaining rights being violated, but the
only economic resource available to this tribe is
being destroyed. The Paiutes of Pyramid Lake
depend on fishing and the issuance of licenses to
sportsmen for their limited income.

The Interior Department has failed to argue for
the Indian claims in court cases, and has refused to
make available to the Paiutes the expertise and the
conservation mandate of their agency. The Department's attitude has been: trust us, our intentions are
good. Nixon's recent Secretary of Interior, Walter
Hickel, became involved in the issue of the Compact. On March 19, 1969, he declared opposition to
the Compact: "It threatens the survival of the
107,000 acre lake in Nevada, located 30 miles from
Reno, and impinges upon the water rights of the
Pyramid Lake tribe of Paiute Indians who own the
lake."

Hickel met with the Paiutes on July 6 to reaffirm
his stand against the Compact. The following day
the Secretary appeared with California Governor
Ronald Reagan and Nevada Governor Laxalt in a
joint press conference where it was proposed that

*An acrefoot is a unit of volume of water covering one acre to
the depth of one foot (43,560 cubic feet).

the Lake be reduced to 70,000 acres in order to "stabilize it." Though transcripts reveal that it was not Secretary Hickel who proposed the reduction, he did agree with the principle. Scientifically speaking, the Lake could be stabilized at *any* level, including the present one. On the question of the legality of such a transaction Mr. Hickel said that it was a "tough" question, referring it to Governor Laxalt who stated: "Our theory is that all waters within the state are subject to appropriation . . . whether the applicant is the Federal Government or not." This statement is part of the intricate process called "instant law."

In summation, the water which might be returned to Pyramid Lake from the Newlands Project was stolen in the first place via the Derby Dam; therefore, there is no extraordinary generosity in plans to return it. The legal issue is more complex, and is hardly a bargaining issue. The water rights of the Paiutes are the responsibility of the federal government as guaranteed in the Winter's Doctrine (Treaty of 1859; Nevada was not admitted to the Union until 1864). It remains to be seen whether the U.S. government will protect these rights above those of Nevada (whose own rights are subject to pre-existing Indian rights) in the coming court battles. Roland Westergard, the Nevada engineer to whom all water applications are submitted, seems to express the general attitude toward Indian rights: "There just isn't enough water to go around."

The Taos Pueblos

The Taos Pueblo claims are just as old, and just as complicated. The Taos Pueblo rests at the foot of a mountain in the Sangre de Cristo range of northern New Mexico. Taos has been the scene of brutal

events in its very long history under both Spanish
and American occupation troops. In Teddy Roosevelt's reign, the Pueblo was also reduced by land
theft in the name of conservation. In 1906, 130,000
acres of Taos' land were removed, placed under the
questionable protection of the new U.S. Forestry
Service, and later were incorporated in the larger
Carson National Forest boundaries. This action was
calculated to affect more than the ecology of the
Pueblo. The lands on which the famous artists'
colony of Taos was built also were *legally recognized* as belonging to the Pueblo.

Under Forestry Service management the tribe
was required to obtain a permit to use its own land
for its age-old religious ceremonies. According to
the Taos leaders, the religion accounts for the unity
and resistance of their people for over 600 years.
The tribe worked to get back its land because it is
holy land. The Blue Lake watershed has always
been its land. The Taos went to court, to Congress,
and to the United Nations once it was organized.
The Taos also went to the Pueblo Lands Board and
offered to forfeit $300,000, owed them for land
within the city of Taos, if the Board would only
recommend that the Sacred Mountain and Blue
Lake shrine be returned to them.

During the administration of President Harding,
Secretary of Interior Albert Fall, by legislative
measures, had moved to strip the Pueblos, and
specifically Taos, of all rights to lands claimed
simultaneously by non-Indians. His efforts were
blocked by the All-Pueblo Council, but then he
resorted to a propaganda campaign of the lowest
kind to defame and bring public opinion to bear
against Indian religious practices. A long, ugly
struggle ensued in which the Indians, supported by
early Indian-rights organizations and other tribes,

fought back calmly and in the end successfully. Secretary Fall was indicted for taking a $100,000 bribe in the famous Teapot Dome Oil scandal, fined the amount of the bribe and sentenced to one year in prison. His supporter, Commissioner of Indian Affairs Charles Burke, continued to lead the religious suppression drive, publishing a 193-page document depicting Indian religions as "foul, pornographic, lewd, savage" ceremonies, which he circulated to newspapers, magazines, churches and women's clubs. Under questioning in a Senate investigation in 1928, Burke accused his own detractors of conspiracy to destroy the BIA and federal authority in Indian affairs. The Senate demanded that he prove these accusations. He could not, and resigned. Although a so-called Indian "New Deal," was instituted by President Franklin D. Roosevelt with the Indian Reorganization Act, the real issue at Taos remained unresolved as the Indians still did not have title to their land.

In 1956 the Indian Claims Commission* confirmed the rights of the Taos to 130,000 acres of land, including the 48,000-acre Blue Lake shrine, offering a substantial cash settlement which the tribe refused. The tribe did not want to sell its land and pressed for legislation in the U.S. Congress for its return.

In Congress, that supreme law-making (and breaking) body of the United States, the wheels of the nation are oiled with easy money. There are lumber lobbies, and oil lobbies, and religion lobbies whose voices demand "equal representation" in our government. There just happens to be a virgin

---

*The U.S. government established the Court of Indian Claims and the Indian Claims Commission in 1946 to adjudicate Indian land claims. Under the law, tribes must apply to the U.S. Congress for permission to sue the U.S. government.

forest on the 130,000 acres of Taos Pueblo land.
Senator Clinton Anderson of New Mexico, who is a
Mormon, has been the prime opponent of Taos land
claims in recent years. He has suggested that their
religion is not as important as the material "interests" of the country, i.e., lumber. He has drawn up
his own legislation in which the Taos will receive
title to 1,600 acres. At hearings he has demanded
that the Indians show him just which parts of their
land are the *most* religious, but they answer that
none is more so than any other. It is all sacred land.

In 1968, Secretary of the Interior Stewart Udall,
showing an unusual understanding of the Taos'
religious needs, testified in favor of the return of the
entire 48,000-acre Blue Lake tract. The legislation
passed the House of Representatives unanimously,
but was killed in the Senate. Under pressure from
this favorable legislation, Anderson offered 3,150
acres for the exclusive use of Taos, but by 1969 the
figure had again dropped to 1,600 acres.

Under the permit of the U.S. Forestry Service,
the people of Taos have maintained their secret
religion. At times the Forestry Service has harassed
the people during their ceremonies, patrolling, in-
truding, and taking photographs like stupid tourists.
The service explains that it is just making sure the
Indians are using their holy land in accordance with
governmental regulations. On the other hand, the
Forestry Service has violated its own regulations by
over-stocking the lakes with fish, then using dyna-
mite to kill the excess fish. It presently uses helicop-
ters to buzz Indians during religious ceremonies.
These methods are not out of character with the
continuing anti-Indian feelings within the Indian
Bureau and the Department of Interior.

In the summer of 1970, President Nixon endorsed
the Taos Land Bill, calling for a new justice for

American Indians. The next day, Senator Anderson managed to kill the bill by keeping it locked in the Committee on Indian Affairs which he heads. In the hearings, Anderson demanded that the Taos Indians reveal all their rites to show the religious necessity for the use of each and every acre of their land, that he might be satisfied none would be wasted if given to them. The Indians refuse to reveal any more of their religion than has been already exposed by prying anthropologists, realizing that that isn't even the issue. Anderson represents lumber companies, and is a Mormon (its beliefs are racist, and anti-Indian).

At long last, on December 2, 1970, the Senate voted 70 to 12 in favor of returning title to the Taos of the entire 48,000 acres of disputed lands, under perpetual trust status. Although one may argue that this is a truly "liberal" gesture, it is not because the land was really not the government's to "give." Simultaneous with this display of "liberal" generosity, the Colville reservation in Washington state was finally terminated, 200,000 acres of land auctioned off to the highest bidding lumber companies.

Pit River Indians

The Pit River Indian tribe in Northern California recently reclaimed its land. Two hundred Indians, in a daring night assault, occupied a portion of their land under lease to the Pacific Gas & Electric Co. (PG&E). After a few days they were arrested and charged with trespassing.

In the middle and late 1850's the United States had made treaties with some California tribes for their land, and had established reservations. However, the lands of other tribes were sold without consultation. In any case most of the treaties were not ratified by Congress, nor were the tribes informed of this fact until after all their lands were already sold.

The California Claims Commission voted to reimburse the tribes, recognizing the ownership of 3,500,000 acres of land by the Pit River tribe alone. But tribes have little use for money of that kind. They want what is theirs, their land. The land "owned" by Pit River is also "owned" and leased by the following corporations: PG&E, the Kimberly Clark Paper Co., California Fruit Growers (Sunkist), Pacific Telephone & Telegraph, Southern Pacific Railroad, Hearst Publications, U.S. Plywood & Champion Papers, Publishers Forest Products (Los Angeles *Times*), and others. It is pointless to ask how they obtained access to this Indian land. It is only reasonable to know why Indians have no rights in the courts.

Presently, the Pit River tribe demands that all corporations immediately vacate its lands, and that all profits earned from the land be turned over to it. The Indians request that subscribers to PG&E services pay their bills to the Pit River tribe. They received about $250,000 and more money is coming in; they insist on a thorough accounting of the books of all corporations involved. They also demand reparations to all California Indians for genocide and enforced poverty during the last 100 years. They want the corporations and the U.S. government to undo the damage done to their land by the building of dams and power lines, railroads and highways, and by the denuding of forests for the paper industry. They demand religious and cultural freedom. Finally, they note that all the demands are inseparable. The proclamation went unpublished in the nation's press.

After the police confrontation, they were represented in court by Aubrey Grossman of San Francisco. In an impressive defense presentation, Mr. Grossman proposed that PG&E and the federal government should be renamed as the defendants, and his clients as plaintiffs. He moved for dismissal of all charges, contested the constitutionality of the prosecution's case and moved to prosecute PG&E. Needless to say, the court saw it in other terms, and refused all the defense motions. In the course of the defense, Mr. Grossman cited three areas in which national responsibility was violated:

(1) By arbitrary and illegal acts deprive a people of the land they have held immemorial, which also is a prerequisite to the satisfaction of their material, spiritual, and religious needs; and

(2) When finally the nation has confessed the illegality of its acts toward the injured people, and announced this confession in the way provided by the laws of the nation, refuses to return the stolen land; and

(3) Arrest and imprison representatives of the injured people when they use self-help to repossess the land which was stolen, and illegally withheld from them for 117 years.

He then concluded:

"At this precise moment in history when all segments of government in the United States, including the President, are excoriating violence and demonstrative actions, and praising and advocating (what they describe as its opposite) 'law and order,' it is not exactly consistent (and some uncharitable commentators might describe it as dishonest, inconsistent, hypocritical, or at least a 'credibility gap') for every agency of government to refuse to enforce a decision of the highest court of the land in favor of the Pit River Indians and then, rubbing salt in the terrible genocidal wounds sustained by Indian people, by arresting and imprisoning them for their self-help—by asserting that they, having waited with true Indian patience for 117 years, have not waited long enough."

The case is still being adjudicated.*

The Passamaquoddy Indians

The Passamaquoddies fought with the colonists in the War of Independence, and were praised by George Washington for their services. Under treaty with the Commonwealth of Massachusetts they retained possession of tens of thousands of acres of land. They were given about 100,000 acres on which to conduct hunting and other traditional activities; the sole privilege of the Commonwealth was the taking of timber suitable for ship masts, with all proceeds from the lumbering to accrue in a "trust" fund for the tribe.

When Maine, where the Passamaquoddy lived, was carved out of the Commonwealth, the treaty was not reaffirmed, though legally there was no need to do so. But Maine did not honor the treaty, nor did Massachusetts carry out its legal responsibilities as set forth in it. Thus, Passamaquoddy land in Maine was soon sold, with proceeds going into the state treasury; lumber was taken in the same way. In more recent years land has been preempted by the State of Maine for a railroad right-of-way and a highway, for which the tribe was not compensated. Today, Indians can only find jobs at the paper mill in Machias which processes Indian lumber. The three Passamaquoddy reserves are deep in poverty. The school system has been

*Since writing this, Indians reoccupied the Pit River land, only to be attacked October 21, 1970 by over 200 California State Police, assisted by Federal Marshals. More than 40 people were injured, and as many people arrested, for merely being on their own land.

run by the Catholic Church for 300 years.

There are always problems with local and state officials, not to mention local citizens. A pregnant woman was dragged by a car driven by a state official, causing her to lose her child—he did not want to hear her protests. Five drunk white deer hunters came onto the reservation at Dana Point, and desiring to rape an Indian's wife and daughters, they entered his home and terrorized his family. He managed to get his family to safety before they cold-bloodedly beat him to death. One was charged with manslaughter; all were acquitted.

State Police continue to harass Indians, stopping, threatening, and brutalizing them. In one recent case, the Indians fought back and successfully interfered with an absurd arrest. The reservation was raided in the night by State Police and deputized game wardens, in an effort to find the Indians of the day's brawl. People were dragged from their houses and kicked and beaten severely. There was a court case against the Indians, though without the results expected by the officials. An inquiry into the police-state policies was requested, and the Governor asked the State Police to investigate itself. The "investigation" showed that no undue brutality was ever used!

With the preparation of the land claims case, other Gestapo techniques surfaced. When Muskie was Governor, there was a program to build houses for the Indians, using the money from the "trust" fund held by the State. Two companies contracted to build the plywood houses, nearly 30 of them, costing between $7,000 and $9,000 apiece. The houses completed, the companies filed bankruptcy papers to avoid prosecution, for the houses began falling apart within a year of their completion. Muskie took this loss out of the Indian trust fund, reducing it to a mere $70,000. For 75 years the tribe had trudged to the State Capitol each year for an accounting of its money. The Indians have never been told exactly how much they had. Now that it is almost gone, though without any accounting to show where, they are told.

When the claims case began, they applied for funds from their own account to pay their lawyer, Don C. Gellers, but officials refused. The claims case went ahead anyway, funded by the Indian Rights Association. The tribe claims 30,000 acres outright ownership: a group of islands, and land long ago sold by the state (Passamaquoddies live on barely 200 acres of their once extensive lands); 395,000 acres of timber land set aside for their economic maintenance; lumber money since 1820, plus interest; compensation for highway and railroad rights-of-way. The claim has been filed by Don C. Gellers and the famous Boston lawyer, John S. Bottomly, in the Massachusetts court in which the treaty was originally completed.

As the claims case was being presented, the state of Maine moved to disbar Mr. Gellers. In a strange drama of cops and spies, he was arrested for possession of marijuana. He was held illegally for two hours away from his house while it was being searched, and then booked. Since the warrant did not have a show-cause clause, the hearing judge moved to suppress the evidence. The State District Attorney has continued to press the case through a series of Alice-In-Wonderland trials. The truth is in the saying: as Maine goes, so goes the nation.

Then, with the claims case going through the tedious court protocol, the Georgia Pacific Lumber Co., one of the largest in the world, became concerned lest the Indians get back their lumber land, then being cut by GP. The company began to bulldoze an area in the forest, and to scrape the land, a procedure that would destroy the forest for about 200 years to come. The Indians protested to no avail. Then, on July 4, 1968, they went on a "picnic" to the cutting site, armed, and wearing Indian clothes. The confrontation was brief. The GP workmen driving the diesels backed down, and the Passamaquoddies let it be known in no uncertain terms that they would not sit by and watch their land be ruined. Meetings of a more official nature followed, with representatives of Georgia Pacific, the State of Maine, and the tribe. The agreement reached was a landmark: Indians would begin to be hired in large numbers for the lumber operation, equipment would be given them to begin to "Indianize" the management of the cutting, and full management would revert to the tribe in 15 years.

In 1969, again on July 4, the Passamaquoddy people at the Pleasant Point reserve closed the highway which goes through their land and began charging a toll. They continued the toll action for several hours, until State Police came and broke it up, arresting several Indians.

Although the Passamaquoddy number only around 800 people, their success can be largely attributed to the unity of their actions, actions planned by their own leadership. Today they suffer an unemployment rate of at least 80 per cent, though this will soon be changed by tribal programs. Few tribes, regardless of numbers, have been as effective in their resistance to "official" theft, and in obtaining reparations for their unjust treatment.

The Alaskan Indians

In Alaska, there is a land issue dating from the transfer of the territory from Russia to the United States. Russia had sought to establish Native title to lands, but, due to the nomadic way of life, was unsuccessful. The sale of the territory in 1867 included a treaty with the United States which stipulated that U.S. citizenship, and implicitly land rights, should be withheld from "the uncivilized native tribes." The Alaskan Organic Act of 1884 ruled that Indians would not be disturbed in their use of the lands, "the term under which such persons may acquire title to such land is reserved for future legislation by Congress." A special Commission was formed to report "what lands, if any, should be reserved for their (Native) use."

The report evolved into the Alaska Native Allotment Act of 1906 which authorized the Secretary of Interior to allot up to 160 acres of non-mineral land to each head of a family. Only 15,000 acres were so allotted, due to the uselessness of such allotments to people dependent on food-gathering and hunting over great areas.

Under Presidents T. Roosevelt and Harding, large areas were withdrawn for mineral and oil exploration. Today 360 million out of the 375 million acres of Alaska belong to the Federal government. There was no attempt by the government to establish any Native claims to the land, nor to meet the demands of the Natives for compensation. The Natives were not consulted by the government about the withdrawal of their lands.

Tribes were stripped of great land holdings. Their sources of livelihood, furs and fishing and hunting, were exploited almost to extinction by the technology of the white man. Seals, salmon, and fur-bearing animals were literally wiped out, first by the Russians, finally by the Americans. The Kenaitzi tribe was stripped of its livelihood, then its lands. The United States decided this land would make a fine moose reserve. When oil was discovered the moose range was opened to drilling and to real-estate developers. Almost two million acres were stolen, leaving the Kenaitzi in the status of squatters.

During the mid 1930's the Eklutnas lost 378,000 acres under the Johnson-O'Malley Act when they were offered their own land as a reservation. They were not informed of the means for accepting the lands, and the land was withdrawn after a short period of time. Anchorage has since sprawled out over their lands, and the Alaska Power Administration has preempted 5,000 acres more. Today the Eklutnas have 1,800 acres on which to live and have to get permits to cut wood on their own land. On the other hand, the Tlingit-Haida tribes were "allowed" to sue the United States in the Court of Claims and did receive $7.5 million for the 18 million acres they had lost. The Tyoniks received $14 million for their lands and have hired outside consultants to develop feasible programs for housing, education, and employment.

In 1966 the Alaskan Native Brotherhood was formed around the land claims issue. It has led the movement for Native rights, and has pushed Congress toward settlement of the issue before further dividing up the Alaskan frontier. The huge oil deposits discovered at Point Barrow, Alaska have made the land claims issue that much more urgent.

In July of 1970, Congress passed the Alaskan Land Bill, granting 40 million acres, 500 million dollars, and most important, a royalty of two per cent on all resources extracted from their lands. All funds were to be administered by a corporation of which the majority were Alaskan Natives. The final version of the bill, with amendments, fell short of these minimal expectations. Native lands were reduced to only 10 million acres; the corporation will not have a majority of Natives; and in June 1971, when the Land-Freeze is lifted by law, Congress has voted to claim whatever land there remains.

The Seminole

In Florida, as in California, the U.S. Claims Commission has recognized Indian title to 80 per cent of the State. The Seminole tribe, though it made treaties with the United States, resisted the "removal" policy and was not defeated in its wars. Thus it never legally signed away its land rights. The Court of Claims estimated the lands to be worth $50 million, but Congress decided to pay only $12 million. All claims are based on land prices at the time they were stolen. The Seminoles have refused the payment, demanding the land. Their tribal leaders have compared the $12 million with the figure of $350 million given by the United States to anti-Castro Cubans.

7

HUNTING AND FISHING RIGHTS

HUNTING AND fishing rights were guaranteed as well in the original treaties with the Indian nations. Yet, Indians have been continually prohibited from exercising these rights. For the Indians hunting and fishing are not merely a form of recreation. Since most reservations are extremely impoverished, these activities are necessary for their very livelihood. Time and again sportsmen and conservationists have restricted the Indians in the pursuit of their very means of subsistence.

In response to the curtailment of their rights, the Indians are waging both legal and extra-legal battles. Some of the combatants have spent as much time in jail as out. Because of the civil disobedience nature of the demonstrations, however, few Indians have been killed. There have been countless times when the behavior of the law enforcement officials has given way to brutality, the beating of children, the kicking of women and the shooting of unarmed young men. Here again, only a few cases will be documented.

Conservationists, heeding the call of the so-called "sportsmen" of America, have succeeded in securing hunting licenses and rights for this strong lobby-group. Yet, Indians continue to hunt deer on their own land without regard to hunting seasons and licensing. In a number of areas, including Oklahoma, South Dakota, Arizona, New Mexico, Idaho, Washington, New York, Maine, North Carolina, Florida, and nearly every other state with deer and Indians, the issue has been unresolved either in court or in the field. Game wardens have sought, unsuccessfully, to prosecute Indian hunters. The issue has been clouded by the claims of conservationists that hunting has to be regulated to protect the species. This argument applies only to the annual slaughter by white men seeking "trophy" animals who often leave killed animals to rot while seeking other, larger specimens to hang on their walls as proof of their "masculinity." Indians do not slaughter deer, nor do they waste meat. Though in general Indians are no longer as conservation-minded as they were once, they hardly pose a threat to the species by their minimal hunting practices. It is the loss of the license fee which irks the National Rifle Association (alias the "Great White Hunter") more than the need to regulate for reasons of conservation.

Indians also depend upon a variety of fish in their diets. The very poor quality of both fish and meat products sold on reservations, makes hunting and fishing an absolute necessity. Laws which in effect tell a man who is hungry that he may not eat must be altered.

The Minnesota Chipewas

In a dispute over licensing, the Solicitor General ruled for the BIA in 1936 that "though hunting rights of the (Minnesota) Chipewa were not written into the treaties, they are still to be upheld by virtue of the larger rights possessed by them on land occupied and used." The customary rights of a tribe remain inviolable unless specifically rescinded in treaties. Thus, the Red Lake tribe of Chipewas was not required to purchase the licenses and migratory bird stamps in order to hunt ducks, geese, etc.

A similar dispute arose over the traditional wild-rice harvest by the Minnesota Chipewas, in which the state sought to regulate by licensing the tribes' rights to the harvest. In 1969 the Chipewas embarked on a series of civil-disobedience actions against the licensing and the curfew being imposed by state officials. Arrests did take place, but the harvest went on essentially undisturbed.

Under similar circumstances, the federal government ruled in 1969 that Indians throughout an eight-state region of the southwest and the Rockies cannot gather pinyon nuts excepting they pay a tax. This harvest has been of economic importance to Indians for centuries, providing many with a major food source, as well as a commercial base. Actions are being planned to oppose this oppressive ruling.

Washington State Indians

In the state of Washington the Indian people have been fishermen for over 30,000 years. They catch the salmon as they move upstream to spawn away from the ocean. From Alaska to northern California, Indians are accustomed to seek the salmon. In the treaties of 1854, between the Columbia river tribes and the U.S. government, the Indians' right to fish was guaranteed although 64 million acres of land were ceded away, reserving only six million acres for the tribes. Both pressure and chicanery were used at these treaty councils. While the Indians were not deprived of their fishing ventures, they were encouraged to take up farming on small homesteads. In fact the Indians had been deliberately misled, for the fishing rights applied only within the reservation boundaries. According to the Medicine Creek treaty of 1854, fishing and hunting "at all usual and accustomed grounds and stations is further secured to said Indians (Nisquallies and Puyallups) . . . ." The treaty of Point Elliott with the Muckleshoot tribe reads exactly the same. The Yakimas, Flatheads, Kutenais, and others were also deprived of land. Since most tribes sincerely did not understand the language in which the thefts were couched, a minor war resulted.

Nevertheless, the reservation system was imposed, and the reduction of the land base continued. Farming ventures were failures, but in a rare show of concern for Indian self-sufficiency, the Indian agents developed a plan to assist the tribal fishing enterprises. However, the plans ran contrary to the age-old policy of the BIA that Indians become farmers, so that they can be brought into the "mainstream" of American life. The fishing activities of the Columbia River and Puget Sound tribes have been severely restricted, as have their land holdings. "Accustomed" fishing places are mostly in the hands of whites, and though early court cases ruled that Indians might cross non-Indian land to reach these stations, the Indians found it often difficult to do so, due to hostility. State regulations have had the greatest effect on the fishing practices of these tribes, and are the basis for much controversy.

In 1913 Indians began being arrested by state authorities for fishing activities, even on their own federally-supervised lands. The Washington fish and game commissions shared responsibility for commercial and sports fishing, and acted under state laws to suppress the Indians. In 1929, Washington state denied the Quinalt tribe the right to fish, choosing to lease their rights to a private company of Baker's Bay for a $36,000 fee. This lease proved to be the issue which sparked the beginning of fishing rights struggles.

State courts have ruled that, based on the testimony of anthropologists, the tribes who signed the treaties no longer exist. In truth, dynamic changes have occurred in Indian cultures, but not those specific changes which were stated by the courts. The Supreme Court has overruled the state court decisions. Even with this overruling, the oppressive police and game warden tactics have continued, resulting in a near state of war.

In order for the state to provide more fishing grounds for sportsmen and private companies, officials have deliberately over-extended the interpretation of Public Law 280, a provision which sets guidelines for the enforcement of state laws on the Indians only with their consent. In 1965, in response to this interpretation, the Indians began a series of civil-disobedience actions called "fish-ins." The new National Indian Youth Council worked with the tribes in a number of fish-ins, bringing in Indians from a score of other tribes across the country. The officials of Washington, in open opposition to Supreme Court rulings, arrested Indians for "illegal" fishing, using tear gas, blackjacks, and excessive violence to subdue two dozen Indian men, women, and children. A series of night attacks by state officials followed, using terrorist tactics against old men and women, and violence against the very young. Many people were hospitalized. These actions extended to other tribes along the winding Columbia River, causing the Yakimas to arm themselves against these illegal state actions. Though the Federal officials responsible to the Indians, from Secretary of Interior Udall down, were requested to commit themselves, they did not take any action. Elsewhere, the anti-Indian campaign focused on threatening fish buyers and "urging" the press not to cover the violent confrontations at the rivers. The early fish-ins were chaotic, riotous events due to the blundering actions of the Gestapo police and the natural response by people who see their respected old people and defenseless children attacked, and their treaties violated.

Behind this recent wave of repression are the problems of maintaining a steady fish population in an ecologically unbalanced environment. But, the problems are not primarily created by the Indian fishermen. Of all fish caught in Washington state, 77 per cent are caught by non-Indian sportsmen. The decrease in the fish population caused by dams and pollution from factory and sewage disposal is the greatest problem. Thus, the few fish that do arrive at the upstream fishing points to spawn are considered vital by conservationists. Yet the Indian fishermen only take seven or eight per cent of the total catch. Are the Indians to forego their treaty rights, not to mention their 30,000-year-old tradition of fishing, to satisfy those who fish for a whim? Treaties provided that there be no actual competition between commercial and Indian fishing. Yet, commercial fishers use radar to detect schools of fish. The state, however, opposes every unbiased study of the fishing problem. It has decided to limit Indians, rather than curb the sportsmen and the companies.

Without a doubt, the Indians pose no substantial threat to the survival of the fish, while the state regulations do pose a survival threat to the Indians. The hunting and fishing rights protests and actions must continue until there is finally an honest review of the situation. Also, in light of recent events, the right of self-defense has become a crucial factor in the character of the dispute, a right which is sure to hold an increasingly important place in Indian struggles.*

*During January of 1971, Hank Adams, the executive director of the Survival of American Indians organization (the official voice of the Fishing rights resistance), was out one night checking the nets on the Nisqually river. Two white men approached the car as he waited for his companion to return from the river. They cursed him and Indians in general and shot him through the open car window with a rifle. Tacoma police requested Hank to submit to various tests to establish whether the gunshot was self-inflicted though the bullet had entered his side. Hank has reaffirmed his willingness to continue the resistance.

8

SELF-DETERMINATION AND SOVEREIGNTY

TODAY, THE methods of resistance to intrusions and encroachments have changed from open warfare to more subtle ways. In the meetings with bureaucrats and advisors who control our lives, there are more frequent confrontations. The "man" does not seem to mind being called "liar," "thief," or even "murderer," as long as his programs ineffectually continue. The BIA official, like the administrators of so many community programs, are not interested in community involvement, nor in the real or meaningful changes his programs might otherwise bring about. He is interested in statistics, paper-successes, and in the rainbow of retirement after a long, tediously boring career. In recent years, however, Indian people have become adamant for changes in this primal, bureaucratic monster. Most students of Indian affairs immediately propose the abolition of the BIA, but Indians have both their own reasons for keeping it (the threat of termination) and their own alternatives. Behind this recent upsurge of activism has been the fundamental demand for Indian self-determination.

Why is self-determination so essential to the Indians? The origins of this demand go back 100 years (to consider recent times only) when they were still free and were successful in their economic endeavors. Indians are different from other peo-

ple. They are culturally different, and they sometimes have opposite values from the "mainstream."
There are religious differences which have in no
way been resolved by the interference and attacks
of the heavy-handed BIA and the 30-odd Protestant
and Catholic missionary groups. There is a body of
U.S. law, setting Indians apart from America and
Americans. It includes 33 volumes of BIA "regulations," 5,000 federal statutes, 2,000 federal court
decisions, and 500 decisions by the U.S. Attorney
General. Yet, government agencies aside from the
BIA, such as the Office of Economic Opportunity,
Community Action Program, Vista, Office of Economic Development Administration and numerous
subsidiary agencies, maintain projects in road-
building and conservation which utilize a considerable area of Indian land. All these projects are for
the benefit of white men. By inviting white development of Indian resources and facilities, these
agencies further the aim of the federal government's Indian policy: the assimilation of the Indian
into the so-called "mainstream" of U.S. economic
life.

Many of the programs designed for the reservations are regarded as "experiments" to be tried out
on the Indians. If the programs are successful, they
will be packaged and "exported" to Africa, Latin
America and Southeast Asia. The agencies responsible for these foreign aid programs include the
BIA, the Public Health Service (pilot projects), and
the Office of Economic Opportunity—all in con-
junction with the Central Intelligence Agency.
Though it would be difficult to document, a com-
parison of the Indian projects with the "packaged"
projects for overseas deployment, including an
examination of U.S. Army military tactics and
massacres and the "relocation" (reservation) camps

used in Vietnam, might very well reveal an amazing similarity of design.*

The continued production of governmental and institutional reports over the last hundred years is itself an indication of the failure of the programs. Considering the minimal changes resulting from the projects, the amount of money consumed in the assessment and reassessment of the research already completed is an intolerable waste. Yet, this squandering of funds continues to be academically justified by those who so ardently seek a solution to the Indian "problem." There is not now, nor has there been, any realistic or honest attempt to solve the problems created for the Indians by the white man. The research done by and for the government, including the meaningless work of the less than sensitive anthropologists, only proves this point. The volumes of Indian records in the U.S. archives, the correspondence between agents and higher officials and the numerous Senate hearings, reinforce every argument that can be made against the government's and American people's concern for equal justice and progress, in Indian terms.

The complete failure of the education programs is appalling. The vicious, brutal treatment of Indian children in the name of American education is nothing less than cultural, or second-degree geno-

---

*During hearings on Vietnam before the Senate Foreign Relations Committee, General Maxwell Taylor is quoted as saying: "But I have often said it is hard to plant corn around the stockade when the 'Indians' are still around . . . . We have to get the Indians farther away in many provinces." One wonders whether the war in Vietnam is not merely the western frontier extended to some warped, "logical" conclusion, a 20th century form of Manifest Destiny. Also, in a Green Beret training manual designed as a comic book, there is a picture of a U.S. soldier killing a Vietcong soldier. The caption reads: "That's one little Indian that won't talk anymore."

cide. The investigations of the recent Senate Subcommittee Hearings on Indian Education are a
shocking revelation of the inadequate teachers and
programs, and of the outright attempts to destroy
the Indian people. The conditions at the numerous
BIA schools, but particularly the Chilocco Oklahoma school, are like a nightmare from Inquisitional
Spain!—children beaten and chained overnight
from ceilings, whose wrists are permanently de-
formed and scarred, jailed in dungeons for minor
infractions, forced to work at hard labor in the
homes of the school officials in the name of "Industrial and Homemaking" training. Following the investigation, the FBI suppressed the proven evidence.

The suppression of Native religion is another
example of cultural genocide. The stealing of objects used in Indian religions for exhibition by
museums and universities is a major source of
ill-feeling among Indians. Were the objects repre-
sentative of dead, rather than active, living religions, there might be no argument. The anthropo-
logical propaganda that Indian and Native religions
are dead merely serves the desired aims of the
government. Likewise, the views held and expressed by would-be Indian "experts" that Indian
tribalism is "obsolete" serve only to assist the
government in achieving its long-hoped-for results.

The confrontations which have occurred during
the last year between Indian activist and church
groups have been of the nature of a religious
challenge. For example, a coalition of Indian organizations is currently attacking the practice of the
missionary boards by which they use funds raised
for Indian programs in other projects. The Indians
urge the Christians to re-evaluate their past actions,
to devise programs only with Indian advisors, to
honestly fund Indian self-help programs, in order

that Christians may "repent" for their sins against the Indian people.

One can imagine the hypocrisy that these Indian spokesmen have encountered. The promises made at the religious conferences for the administration of Indian programs by Indian boards and for greatly increased funding of projects have led to absolutely nothing. It would seem that the American Christian cannot even follow his Commandment *thou shalt not lie.* It is the policy of the church leadership to lie in the numerous publications on church activities, as it is the policy of the Christian churches to be racist by refusing voting rights to Indian ministers at national meetings, though Black ministers have to a degree achieved these rights. Few members of these churches (Lutheran, Methodist, Baptist, Evangelical, Mormon, Catholic) have any more understanding of the necessity of Indian self-sufficiency and self-determination than do the government officials "in charge" of Indian Affairs. For too long they have cooperated, to an astounding degree, with the colonialist BIA. They have benefited from it financially by receiving money from the trust funds of "illiterate" Indians at the legal disposal of Department of Interior officials. This complicity is now known and will no longer be tolerated. We do not recognize the right of the federal government, nor the numerous interests of Christianity, to do with our people as they, in their racist vision of superiority, see fit.

It is amazing that people continue to suggest that we should "work through the existing system." It is a difficult thing these people ask and something they themselves could not possibly understand. The system we are told to support was founded on greed, violence and injustice, and persists under those very same terms. It will receive less and less cooperation from Indian people as the facts, so well hidden from the public, are finally understood. It is already fully documented that the government has destroyed almost every successful Indian project based on self-sufficiency and self-determination and that those tribes who have achieved some independence have done so on their own terms.

The demands by numerous tribal governments for more active participation in the control of their resources and institutions are finally bringing about what 100 years of political promises have failed to achieve. But these achievements are taking far too long, and in some cases are coming too late to succeed at all. The tribes whose resources are being left purposefully undeveloped are in the worst situations. The greedy entrepreneurs of natural resources anxiously wait for the tribes to be economically strangled into selling their lands and resources. It is no accident that during 1970 alone more than 200,000 acres of reservation lands passed from Indian ownership. Most of this land is on the west coast, mostly forest lands, quickly obtained by the largest lumber companies, with the assistance of the BIA, the Department of Interior and Congress. On other reservations the land and resources are sold bit by bit, eliminating the only means by which the tribes can survive economically. The tribal governments under the authority of the BIA have little to say in these matters. Although these governing bodies are elected by the members of the tribe, the elected Indians are subject to the "approval" of the Department of the Interior. The governing bodies should be endowed with more authority to carry out the business of their nations.

Each new White House administration and numerous Senators will promise changes in the policies of Indian administration. This we feel is absurd. To change the BIA would require dismissal of all personnel on the secretarial and office-staff levels and the replacement of a considerable portion of present department heads by Indians. The funds presently consumed in redundant salaries should be going directly to the Tribal Councils, on contract with the U.S. government, if necessary, so that they can run their own programs. We have learned through the decades of meaningless dialogues with officials ("You people aren't ready yet to manage your own lives") that the Indian problem remains a white problem; that we, like others in America, will be recognized as equals only when we force the issue. But Indians are not pushy. We are not the innate savages we are represented as being; were we so, none of this would have happened. The necessary changes in the resistance and demands by Indians are just coming to the surface. Many people just do not understand. "That isn't the way Indians are," I'm told time and time again by anthropologists, missionaries, and other "Indian experts." It may not be Indian behavior, certainly not those qualities that we ourselves admire, to shout, to be rude, and to demand; but it is the only way we will ever be heard. It is the only way the officials and politicians and exploiters will let us be heard. It is that way, or it is back to war again.

As an outgrowth of the occupation of Alcatraz, a unique series of Indian actions occurred during 1970 over the issues of inadequate services and job discrimination in the BIA. Beginning in March 1970 (the same week that Fort Lawton in Washington State and Ellis Island in New York Harbor were being occupied), BIA offices were occupied and subsequently closed down until a hearing took place between Indians and high government officials.

Several meetings did take place. In the Littleton, Colorado offices, Assistant Secretary of Interior Loesch met with the occupying Indians after which he ordered them removed by force and arrested for trespassing on federal property. Occupations occurred in the BIA offices in Chicago and Cleveland, and a demonstration took place at a Gallup, New Mexico, BIA warehouse.

Were it the policy of the BIA, or the U.S. government to secure for Indians the self-determination that would be a step toward "assimilation" in the American mainstream, they would include Indians in the administration of the BIA. Yet, except for a number of figureheads and "tokens" it has been the policy to hire only whites. Out of a budget of a mere $525 million for the fiscal year 1970, not including funds from the Public Health Service, the Office of Economic Opportunity and the Community Action Program, the BIA maintains a staff of 50,000 non-Indians. This staff "serves" 600,000 reservation Indians. On the other hand, there are only 16,000 Indians in government service, few who are in Indian affairs. Those hired by the BIA usually serve as janitors and secretaries. If the BIA is to continue, it must begin to recruit available Indian leaders to fill jobs. If the government is honestly to seek Indian self-sufficiency and determination, the programs must be Indian-designed. The only really successful tribal developments have been those under tribal management. Indians neither trust nor cooperate willingly with white-oriented "plans" for their future. This very basic fact is forever ignored by officials who believe that if a project succeeds on paper, that is good enough, and who forget that it is supposed to be government policy to have members of minority groups service their own peoples.

The demand for self-determination extends to every aspect of Indian oppression and is the basis of a nationalist and activist movement which is growing at an unprecedented rate. It is within this movement that the aims and goals of the Indian people are being formulated: self-determination, free practice of Indian religions, and the recognition of Indian sovereignty. In order to realize these goals, it is necessary that the Indians be granted their rights in full, assume complete control of all facilities and resources belonging to them and bring about a meaningful reorganization of the BIA.

The Indian movement is aware of the international aspect of its struggle. Presently, under the rights of a sovereign nation, application is being made by one Indian nation for admission to the United Nations, and a legal case is being brought against the United States and Canada by an Indian nation in the World Court. The Indians, who have occupied Alcatraz Island in San Francisco Bay for over a year under an 1868 Sioux treaty granting Indians first rights to government surplus lands, are sounding out the possibility of receiving "foreign aid" from countries other than the United States. Having been schooled in the international politics of the 15th through the 18th centuries, Indians have learned the difficulties of international diplomacy. The time is near when a greater involvement is to be expected in this realm.

In a time in which unity in the form of coalitions is occurring between dissimilar groups, it is imperative to recognize the minority and third-world peoples on the North American continent. Although the government "legally" recognizes only those Indians who have been registered with a tribe on a reservation (600,000), there may be as many as 5 million off-reservation Indians, including the Chicano population, who can claim direct Indian descent.* Many of the Chicanos were Indians enslaved by the Spanish, and later by the Americans, to work on the missions and ranches throughout the southwest. Many were Indians from Mexico, sold over the border. Others were Navahos, Apaches, and Indians throughout the southwest and the west coast. Still others were from the west coast of Mexico, of the Yaqui resistance which was defeated by means of kidnapping and deportation.

The Chicanos are engaged in a movement for the land that was granted to them by the Kings of Spain during the 17th and 18th centuries. These extensive properties in New Mexico, Arizona, and Colorado are controversial issues, not only between the Chicano movement and the U.S. government, but between certain Indian tribes and the Chicanos. The Indian point of view is that these lands were originally unceded Indian lands, stolen and then granted to others. Much of the land, though, is not

---

*It is estimated by many Indian authorities that the total Indian population in the United States is far greater than the official figures would indicate. Vine Deloria Jr. estimates at least one million; Mel Thom estimates 1.5 million; more realistically, Jack Forbes estimates 5 million people of Indian descent. This last figure includes Chicanos, and Indians whose tribes were destroyed by Spain, England and the United States. Not all of these people are full-blooded Indians. However, the concept of half-breeds and quarter-bloods is a white man's distinction. In 1960, the U.S. government designated 551,669 people as "official" Indians. Of these, less than one-half are full-blooded. From our point of view, the issue is one of quality of Indian indentification and not quantity of Indian blood. The presence of all Indian peoples in the movement for Indian rights is the significant and vital issue. For example, in the 1830's, when the Cherokees were forced westward, our chief John Ross vigorously opposed this policy. He was only one-eighth Cherokee while many leaders who agreed to removal were more pure-blooded Cherokees.

actually contested by the southwestern tribes. The Chicano movement, led first by Reies Tijerina, occupied land in northern New Mexico, and attacked a town in the summer of 1967. This action, which led to his arrest, brought quick attention to the movement. The Chicanos are running candidates for local and state offices in California, Colorado, Texas and New Mexico. The United Farmworkers Union led by Cesar Chavez is composed primarily of Chicanos. Both the Chicano and Indian movements are struggling against the same forces. There is a need for unity among these oppressed peoples.

As the government of the United States attempts to continue, by use of force, the ridiculously nearsighted colonialism of the past, based on racist capitalism, it seems inevitable that it must fail, just as it already has elsewhere. It would do well to consider the part to be played by the American Indians in the future, and to understand that their role must be their own decision. Any attempts to "sell" Indians on different forms of foreign colonialism will meet with failure. It is unrealistic to expect Indians to choose a new colonialism when they still remain under an old colonialism. And until that fact is recognized there can be no dialogues of any significance. The full recognition of Indian rights, sovereignty, and self-determination must be achieved once and for all, regardless of other so-called national issues. Otherwise, Indian resistance will continue as in the past.

9
INDIAN ORGANIZATIONS

SEVERAL GROUPS and organizations have been active over the years in the struggle for Indian rights. Today the organizations are growing very fast. New groups are forming where Indians have previously appeared to be unpolitical, and coalitions between already established groups are being accomplished. Through the use of modern communications techniques, the existence and aims of the various groups, as well as the actions in which they are involved, are disseminated nationwide. These organizations function in very different ways, fulfilling local, tribal, urban, political, religious, traditional, legal or lobbying needs.

All organizations are ultimately affiliated with tribal groups and needs. The traditional and tribal voice in Indian politics creates the unity and efficacy only obtained elsewhere through decades of activity. Thus Indian organizations have become significant and effective on a national scale in a shorter time than similarly oriented groups.

Indian organizations that were not originally formed or headed by Indians have existed for a long time. During a difficult period of Indian affairs, these groups, the Indian Rights Association, the Concerned Boston Citizens, the American Indian Defense Association, the National Council of American Indians, and other such white-run organizations, did attempt to fight for the rights they felt were due to the Indian people. We do not reject assistance of this sort from sincerely concerned people. Yet, the paternalism manifested by these groups of non-Indian people in the formulation of laws and legislation "for" us is no longer desired. In trying to help us to assimilate painlessly into the "mainstream" society, the paternal white man does a disservice that he is too often unaware of. In his desire to "help the poor Indian," he tries to achieve compromises which have not been any more desirable to the majority of Indians than the more blatant attempts to achieve the same colonialist ends. It is the weakest excuse to preclude Indian action when non-Indian, Indian experts consider that they are more able to speak for the Indian people than Indians themselves. Thus the role played by these early organizations is diminishing to one of supporting and sometimes advising the actual Indian-organized and run groups.

One of the old, paternalist groups deserves special mention: the American Indian Fund (formerly the Association on American Indian Affairs). This body, even with its newly expanded board of Indian directors, is a prototype for such groups. Previously, the AAIA is known to have received federal funds to carry out programs of the BIA which were of no benefit to Indians. Yet, this group has a fine reputation among its non-Indian constituency. In New York City, it runs the American Indian Arts Center which capitalizes on traditional Indian arts and crafts by selling Indian-made goods at up to a 1,000 per cent mark-up. In Congress, the non-Indian head of the organization has continually lobbied in the name of Indians for programs, legal issues, and education with an influence hard to equal by Indians themselves. The AAIA is suspected of collusion with the BIA in the child adoption programs, through which Indian children are literally stolen from their families. The lawyers appointed by the AAIA to settle Indian claims have too often resorted to compromises which are disadvantageous to the tribes involved. In spite of these questionable practices, the prestige and power of the AAIA have not lessened.

Probably the largest and most widely known of the Indian-run organizations is the National Congress of American Indians. The NCAI was formed following World War II, and presently has offices in both Denver and Washington, D.C. Its membership is primarily composed of tribes, of which there are about 183 presently represented. Individual and organizational membership is also available. The function of NCAI is primarily to lobby for or against specific legislation, and to assist tribes in developing a meaningful degree of self-sufficiency on the reservation and community level. The successes of NCAI can not be minimized; however, certain important issues have been ignored because their radical and controversial nature is a threat to the overall tribal body. The NCAI has nevertheless played a most significant role in helping to create the consciousness behind the current political actions of the more activist groups.*

As a result of the "relocation" program of Dillon S. Myer (Secretary of Interior under Eisenhower), there are now probably 250,000 Indians living primarily in the slums and ghettos of Chicago, Minneapolis-St.Paul, Denver, Rapid City, Santa Fe, Los Angeles, San Francisco-Oakland, and Seattle. The organization of Indian Centers in these areas, even in New York (the Southeast Council Federated Eastern Indian League Center, located in Brooklyn's Oceanhill area), has proved important in terms of serving the cultural needs of people no longer in the tribal and reservation setting. The Indian Cen-

---

*Another group serving Indian people in a similar way is the League of Pan-American Indians which studies and reports on illegal activities in claims settlements, and leads in the movement for traditional Indian unity.

ters also engage in direct political action as typified by the San Francisco Center in its relation to the Alcatraz Island occupation, and the Seattle Welcome House during the attempt to occupy Fort Lawton in Washington State.

Within several U.S. and Canadian prisons new organizations are emerging for the purpose of self-help and rehabilitation of Indian prisoners, who are otherwise not provided with rehabilitation facilities. The San Quentin Indian Cultural Group and the Vancouver Halfway House serve the important function of keeping Indians out of prison once they are paroled. The United States provides no similar program.

The involvement of the young in the problems of their people is growing each day, as more Indians seek a meaningful and traditional connection with the solutions already proposed. The National Indian Youth Council (NIYC), one of the first youth-oriented organizations, is made up primarily of Indian college students who oppose the paternalism and exploitation of the BIA. It has continued to grow, and has remained outspoken throughout a decade of activist expression. It has no small number of positive programs to its credit, particularly in the field of Indian education. During the middle and late 1960's a number of similar groups were organized, including the United Native Americans, Native Alliance for Red Power in Canada, Young American Indian Council, Organization of Native American Students, and the American Indian Movement. The last group, AIM, deserves special attention.

AIM was begun in Minneapolis by a group of young Chipewa Indians who had found the other local Indian groups to be too "Uncle Tom," or "Apple" (red on the outside, white on the inside), as we now call them, and unsuccessful in bringing about necessary changes. They first organized the American Indian Patrol to begin photographing and witnessing arrests of Indians in the Minneapolis Indian ghetto, advising them and appearing in court on behalf of those arrested. Using walkie-talkies, cameras, tape-recorders and similar equipment, the Indian Patrol was as mobile and versatile as the police. The immediate effect was a curtailment of police harassment and brutality in their area. The Patrol was also successful in several court cases involving arrested Indians.

In another area, AIM has confronted the missionary boards concerning the exploitation of Indian people, particularly by the Evangelists (Billy Graham) and the Lutherans. These actions have led to take-overs of church facilities in Sioux Falls, South Dakota, and confrontations with Billy Graham from which he has backed down. AIM has started affiliate bodies, as in the Qualla reservation in North Carolina and Cleveland's AIM (CLAIM), and has moved onto reservations considered forbidden to activists up to now. There are currently about 15 groups affiliating with AIM on a national scale, which are involved with the most far-reaching changes attempted anywhere to date, in the fields of industry, alcoholism, housing, communications, etc. In the two brief years of AIM's existence, it has become the most substantial activist group on the continent serving the Indian people.

The final group of organizations, but the most important from the point of view of Indian people, are the tribes. The Indian Reorganization Act of the middle 1930's established the right of tribes to incorporate with the U.S. government. Most tribes did so, and are now legally bound to the government. Yet the real concept of the tribe as a nation is far more comprehensive. It is a concept which has not been legally abandoned, but rather is reinforced by the legal incorporation proceedings, though in terms of white law. In the areas in which the greatest resistance is occurring, organizations have been formed on a tribal basis. The fishing-rights disputes are carried on by the Survival of American Indians organization. On Alcatraz there is the Indians of All Tribes organization. Many years ago the Alaskan people formed into the Alaskan Federation of Natives, the Alaskan Native Brotherhood, and similar groups. There are other organizations serving particular groups of tribes in their fight for their rights: The All-Pueblo Council in the southwest; the United Sioux Tribes in the Dakotas; the United Southeast Tribes in the Gulf states; the pre-Columbian Powhattan Confederacy presently being re-formed on the east coast; and the venerable League of the Six Iroquois Nations in New York State and Canada. All these groups have arisen during extreme times to counteract the forces bent on destroying the Indian people, and they have succeeded in defeating the exploitative policies. The groups are planning their own futures along the lines of self-determination and sovereignty. I think most Indians understand the law of liberation from colonialism: to gain independence, one must fight for it.

Indian leadership, having its share of the usual figureheads, is traditionally determined by individual performance. We only follow a person whose leadership we need and respect, refusing recognition whenever the leader can no longer meet the needs of all involved. A chief may last only one day or for a lifetime. Similarly, leadership may be of either sex. Indian women, for all their alleged submissiveness, have always held greater equality than her white sisters, both in war and peace. In Indian organizations and tribes women hold many responsible positions. Notable Indian women leaders are: Tillie Walker, for many years the outspoken head of the United Scholarship Service; Betty May Jumper, president of the Seminole tribe; councilwoman Anne Wauneka of the Navahos; Kahn-Teneta Horn of the Mohawk resistance; and many others.

Few illusions remain for American Indians. There is the task of educating the people along the lines of resistance in their own terms. The numerous Indian newspapers do this job, as does the American Indian Traveling College in its travels throughout the continent, and the White Roots of Peace, whose message is one of the purest Indian voices to be heard. The issue is not one of power, red or otherwise, but of nations. Those who tell us there will be a "backlash" are jesting. We have survived one of the longest backlashes in history. We have survived the calculated genocide of psychotic Europeans. And our strength is returning, slowly, but most assuredly.

BIBLIOGRAPHY

Akwesasne Notes, Indian Newspaper, Rooseveltown, N.Y.

Americans Before Columbus, National Indian Youth Council, Berkeley, (Nov., 1969).

American Indian Movement Annual Report (1969-1970), Minneapolis.

Andrist, Ralph K., *The Long Death,* Macmillan Co., N.Y., 1964.

Bourne, Edward G. and Olson, Julius E., eds., *Early Narratives of American History,* Scribners & Sons, N.Y., 1906.

Burlage, Robb, "Why We Are in Alaska," in *Hard Times,* Washington D.C., (Nov., 1969).

Clark, David W. and Elizabeth M., *Rehabilitation Program of the Cheyennne River Sioux Reservation,* Indian Rights Association, Philadelphia, 1961.

Collier, John, *Indians of the Americas,* Mentor Books, Chicago, 1947.

——————, *On the Gleaming Way,* Sage Books, Denver, 1962.

Drinnon, Dick, *The Winning of the West,* unpublished manuscript, Bucknell Univ., 1969.

Every, Dale Van, *Disinherited,* Avon Books, N.Y., 1966.

Forbes, Jack, *The Indian in America's Past,* ed., Prentice Hall, Inc., Englewood Cliffs, N.J., 1964.

——————, *Native Americans of California and Nevada,* Naturegraph, Calif., 1968.

Gessner, William, *Massacre,* privately printed, 1931.

Hearings Before the Subcommittee of the Committee on Indian Affairs (1929), United States Papers.

"Hickel and the Press." in *The Sentinel,* National Congress of American Indians, (Convention, 1969).

Hinman, George W., *American Indians and Christian Missions,* privately published, 1933.

Hough, Henry W., *Development of Indian Resources,* World Press, Denver, 1967.

Howard, Helen A. and McGrath, Dan A., *War Chief Joseph,* Bison Books, Univ. of Nebraska, 1941.

Kahn, Edgar, ed., *Our Brother's Keeper: The Indian in White America*, Citizens Advocate Center, Community Press, Cleveland and N.Y., 1970.

Laraque, Marie-Helene, *Destruction of the Indians of the Caribbean*, unpublished manuscript, 1968.

Lockwood, Frank, *The Apache Indians*, Macmillan Co., N.Y., 1938.

Morrison, Samuel, *Admiral of the Ocean Sea*, Little, Brown & Co., Boston, 1942.

Movitz, Deborah, "The Case of the Alaskan Native," in *Civil Rights Digest*, (Summer 1969).

Neihardt, John G., *Black Elk Speaks*, Bison Books, Lincoln, 1931.

Novak, George, *Indian Genocide*, Pathfinder Press, N.Y., 1970.

Nye, William S., *Plains Indian Raiders*, Univ. of Oklahoma Press, 1968.

"Passamaquoddy Indians," in *Ramparts Magazine*, (March, 1967).

Passamaquoddy Tribe vs. The Commonwealth of Massachusetts, (Collection of the author).

People of the State of California vs. Mickey Gimell, Raymond Lego, Charles Buckskin, Richard Oakes, et al., (Collection of the Author).

Preliminary Report, Passamaquoddy Indian Conditions, Maine Advisory Committee, United States Civil Rights Commission.

"Pyramid Lake," in *The Sentinel*, National Congress of American Indians, (Winter-spring 1969).

Sandoz, Mari, *Crazy Horse*, Bison Books, Lincoln, 1942.

Spicer, Edward H., *Cycles of Conquest*, Univ. of Arizona Press, 1962.

Stiener, Stan, *The New Indians*, Harper & Row, N.Y., 1968.

"Taos," in *The Sentinel* (July 1970).

Tundra Times, Alaskan Federation of Natives (June 1970).

Uncommon Controversy: Fishing Rights of the Muckshoot, Puyallup, and the Nisqually Indians, Friends Service Committee, Univ. of Washington Press, Seattle, 1970.

United States Senate Report: Indian Education, Committee of Labor and Public Welfare, 9 volumes, 1968–1970.

The Warpath, Berkeley, United Native Americans, 1969.

Wright, Muriel H., *A Guide to the Indian Tribes of Oklahoma*, Univ. of Oklahoma Press, 1951.

Zelnick, Robert, "Alaska: the Oil Rush 1970," *New York Times Sunday Magazine* (March 1, 1970).

ABOUT THE AUTHOR

WILLIAM MEYER, whose Indian name is *'yonv'ut'sisla* (Burning Bear), is an Eastern Cherokee born in Georgia in 1938. He has studied at Colorado College, Cooper Union and the Art Students League, majoring in engineering and art. His paintings and sculptures have been exhibited extensively, and he has worked as a theatrical engineer. He taught or lectured on the American Indian heritage and related themes at NYU, Brooklyn College, Hunter, Columbia, Bucknell and Alternate U., New York.

Active in the Native American rights struggle since 1956, he has been an officer of the Young American Indian Council and the American Indians-United and a member of numerous other Indian organizations. His activities include constant Congressional lobbying on behalf of Indian land and other claims, work in Indian community projects and in national campaigns such as the effort to save James White Hawk from the death penalty and support for the Alcatraz occupation. He has visited Indian reservations and communities throughout the country.

As writer and journalist, he contributes to an Indian press service and has worked on two reports—*Hunger and Malnutrition USA* and the Citizens' Advocate Center's *Our Brother's Keeper*. He has a forthcoming book with Doubleday, *American Indians Under Christianity: The Suppression of Native American Religion, 1850–1970.*